S15419
618.92   Hyde, Margaret O.
HYD   Cancer in the young
        Cancer in the young

                        8.95

        $8.95

DATE			

Cancer in the Young

Cancer in the Young

A Sense of Hope

by Margaret O. Hyde
and Lawrence E. Hyde

The Westminster Press
Philadelphia

The poem by Marne Beckmeyer in chapter 7 is reprinted from the Candlelighters Childhood Cancer Foundation *Youth Newsletter,* IV, I (Spring 1984) and is used by permission.

Book design by Christine Schueler

First edition

Published by The Westminster Press®
Philadelphia, Pennsylvania

PRINTED IN THE UNITED STATES OF AMERICA
9 8 7 6 5 4 3 2

Library of Congress Cataloging in Publication Data

Hyde, Margaret Oldroyd, 1917–
    Cancer in the young.

    Bibliography: p.
    Includes index.
    SUMMARY: Discusses various types of childhood cancers, their treatment, and prognosis for recovery. Also considers camps, trips, entertainment, and support groups that exist for young cancer patients and their families.
    1. Cancer—Juvenile literature.   2. Tumors in children —Juvenile literature.   [1. Cancer]   I. Hyde, Lawrence E. II. Title.
RC263.H93 1985   618.92′994   84–27126
ISBN 0–664–32722–2

To *Jean Ankeny*
and
Sara McCracken Wright

Contents

1
Cancer in the Young

For children with cancer, there is a new sense of hope. Half the children who are diagnosed this year as having cancer will probably be cured of their disease and be able to go on living productive lives.

This has not always been true. In times past, most children with cancer were condemned to a painful and dismal existence and expected to succumb to their disease either almost immediately or in the not-too-distant future.

There is a new perception of childhood cancer. This does not mean that the picture is entirely bright. Many children with cancer will still die soon after the diagnosis or within the following few years. Those who pass the five-year mark have a good chance of living a normal life span, but a small percentage of these children will develop cancer again. The sense of hope comes from the knowledge that, over all, children with cancer now have a much better chance of living a longer life than ever before.

Childhood cancer is a group of diseases with widely different outlooks for cure. A child's future depends on such variables as the age of the child, the site of the cancer, the stage at which it is diagnosed, the effectiveness of the initial therapy, the attitude of the child, the support of family and friends, and many other factors.

Actually, cancer is rare in children. Only about 3 or 4 out of every 100,000 children die from cancer in a year, but even though the disease is rare, it is second on the list of causes of death for children in the three- to fourteen-year age bracket. About five times as many children lose their lives because of accidents. But cancer remains a dreaded disease for people of all ages and one that seems especially grim when it claims children as its victims.

Can something be done to help the children who suffer from cancer? Can some of these lives be saved? What progress is being made? The American Cancer Society reports that more than 75 percent of the children who have cancer in the United States are being effectively treated, compared with less than 25 percent in 1971. Although some children die sooner than need be because there is a lack of knowledge about symptoms, or because they do not reach medical centers where the best kind of treatment is available, continued research is helping to increase the length and quality of the lives of most of these children.

Christy Smith is just one example of a child whose life has been saved by experimental treatment. Christy went to the Johns Hopkins Oncology Center in Baltimore, Maryland. Similar stories can be told about children at many other hospitals where oncologists—cancer specialists—are working toward better treatments.

Some years ago, Christy awoke with a severe pain in the left side of her body near her ribs. Within days, doctors found that she had a large tumor there that was a form of nerve cell cancer. When the discovery was made, children with this kind of cancer were estimated to have a 5 percent chance of living a normal period of time.

During the next year, Christy endured seven operations, along with other treatments that caused much pain and many unpleasant side effects. During every operation, doctors removed more tumor cells. Then they followed the operation with drug therapy in their efforts to kill other cancer cells in her body. Every time, the cancer cells returned.

Christy was sick much of the time during her treatment. She lost weight, dropping from 92 pounds to 50 pounds. She lost her hair three times, a side effect of her treatment. She was nauseated, vomiting for days after each new set of drug treatments.

As a last resort, doctors suggested an experimental approach in an effort to stop Christy's cancer. After two months of this new treatment, all signs of her cancer were gone. Years later, she remained in normal health, enjoying teenage activities and looking forward to a healthy future.

Not all patients are so lucky, but progress in the fight against cancer has been made on many fronts during the last few decades. Since the 1950s, death rates of children with cancer have fallen as follows: from leukemia, 50 percent; from lymphoma, 32 percent; from bone cancer, 50 percent; from kidney cancer, 68 percent. Deaths caused by other kinds of childhood cancer are down by 31 percent. The five-year survival rate can range as high as 96 percent for thyroid cancer and 80 percent for eye tumors.

Many scientists believe that they are on the threshold of a whole new set of advances in their treatment of cancer. Although they do not foresee a vaccine against cancer in the near future, researchers may soon learn why some people are susceptible to cancer while others are not. This knowledge may lead to ways of building up the body's resistance to cancer before it strikes, allowing a greater rate of cure than at present.

Some experts claim there will never be a cure for all cancers and that cancer will continue to strike in approximately three out of four families. Many of these people will be older family members, but some will be children. Opinions vary greatly as to the chances for greatly improved cancer detection and treatment, but most experts acknowledge good progress as far as children are concerned.

As long as children continue to suffer from cancer, the battle is not over. For the families of the children who die, and for all who live through the cancer experience, there is a long list of serious problems to be faced.

This book deals with cancer as a disease, or many diseases: the facts vs. the myths about cancer; the symptoms and treatment of cancer in children; the feelings, and especially the courage, of these children; and the reasons for a sense of hope for their future.

2
From Cancer Phobia to Facts

Cancer often makes the headlines when a parade of chemicals that may play a part in causing the disease is reported. The parade seems endless. But many leading cancer experts think that the fear of cancer-causing agents, with the exception of tobacco, is an overreaction. While the fear of cancer is reaching epidemic proportions, much of that fear is misguided. No one denies that cancer is a serious life-threatening disease. In the last few years, significant amounts of natural carcinogens (cancer-causing chemicals) have been found. There is strong evidence that at least 116 chemicals or processes can cause cancer, but no one knows just how much or how often they play a part in the development of human cancers. Cancer takes a long time to appear after a person has been exposed to a cancer-causing substance, and scientists often disagree about whether or not the effects of chemicals on test animals such as mice are the same as on humans. Although there seem to be new cancer scares almost daily, experts feel that none of the carcinogens can begin to compare with the impact of tobacco. Since some scientists agree that there may be a sudden increase of chemically caused cancer in the future, caution in the use of known carcinogens seems wise.

Cancer phobia, so common today, has a strong influence on the way people react to others who develop the disease. Suppose you have two friends who have cancer. The boy isolates himself and will not talk about his disease. The girl tells everyone she meets that she has cancer and seeks sympathy for her condition. Neither approach is helpful to them or to other people. Each friend is making the most of some of the myths about a cancer. Johns Hopkins studies of adolescents with cancer show that the vast majority of them undergo significant changes in their appearance and disruption in their daily lives as a result of treatment. Yet, in spite of these pressures, most patients function quite well. Knowledge about cancer, however, can help children and adolescents when they are ready to return to school and society.

Some people are so terrified by the thought of cancer that they cannot think clearly about the disease. They are afraid to be near someone who has cancer just in case it might be catching, so they isolate their ill friends at a time when support is especially needed. They think, wrongly, that *anyone* who has cancer is soon going to die. It is true that some people who have cancer do die shortly after the disease is diagnosed, but in many kinds of cancer the outlook for recovery is good. And there are very few forms of cancer that cannot be slowed by drugs.

Today, utter despair about many kinds of cancer has been replaced by feelings of great optimism. Although new cases of cancer in children occur at the same rate as in earlier years, more of these children are becoming long-term survivors.

The cure rate for some kinds of cancer is quite high. For example, skin cancer patients have an almost 100-percent survival rate. Pat is a fifteen-year-old who has cancer. She spent many hours on the beach, year after year, sunning herself until her skin turned from a bright red to a beautiful dark tan. She liked the look of health it gave her. Several months ago, Pat noticed a rough spot on her arm that did not heal. At first, she was not concerned about it, but after reading the danger signals of cancer on a chart in the library, she decided to check with her doctor.

After Pat's doctor examined the painless sore on her arm, he sent her to a dermatologist, who made some tests and told her that she had skin cancer. On hearing this, Pat panicked until the doctor assured her that almost all cases of skin cancer can be treated successfully. The chance that cancer cells had spread was very slight, but the doctor was very firm about the importance of avoiding sunburn.

Pat had developed a kind of cancer of which the symptoms can be seen in the very early stages. The spot on her arm was removed surgically, and before long Pat was more concerned about the small scar on her arm than about the fact that she had cancer. However, she respected the disease enough to wear a hat when she went outside on sunny days and to lie under a beach umbrella at the shore. She also joined the intelligent people who try gentle tanning or the use of cosmetics to give the so-called healthy look.

There are many myths about cancer that make the very word frightening. Fortunately, the truth is not usually as bad as the myths. One mother who somehow believed that just hearing that someone had cancer would upset her young children was heard spelling the word "cancer" in front of them, but she talked freely about heart attacks. She was probably unaware that many more people die from heart attacks than from cancer. This same fear of cancer prevents some people from seeing a doctor when they discover a symptom. Such a delay accounts in part for the more than 100,000 unnecessary deaths from cancer each year in the United States alone.

Telling the truth about cancer and helping to demystify the disease may play a part in preventing tragedies by encouraging people who suspect they may have it to go for medical examinations. People who are aware that cancer is not contagious are more apt to see a doctor if they recognize a warning signal. They are also more apt to help another person who has cancer.

15

Unfortunately, it is difficult for some people to believe that cancer is not catching. At least one recovered cancer patient has reported having been served with a paper cup while others at a party were drinking from glasses. When the hostess apologized, she said she felt sure the victim understood. Obviously she was ignorant of the fact that cancer is not a contagious disease. She probably was also unaware that millions of individuals have recovered from cancer and that many of them enjoy more energy and enthusiasm than the neurotic or ignorant people who worry about getting the disease.

This unrealistic and overwhelming fear of cancer, called cancer phobia, can be experienced by people in any walk of life. "I have cancer and you won't tell me," is a statement that is often heard in a doctor's office. This may be the case for some patients, even though they have been told by a number of doctors that there is no reason for their fears. One patient who suffered from cancer phobia was a doctor himself. He was so certain that he had cancer of the throat he visited every other physician in town. After each one reassured him, he would feel safe for a while; then his anxiety would mount and he would swab and spray his throat. Finally, one doctor took some cells from his throat and showed the physician the slide that was made from them. When he peered at them through a microscope, the cancer-phobic doctor saw only normal cells. Then he groaned and said, "You substituted a normal slide to spare me the truth."

Not many people suffer from such extreme fear of cancer, but almost everyone worries at some time or other about the possibility of having the disease. Hearing of cases in which people have had good reports from physical examinations and then discover a short time later that they have cancer that has spread to many organs adds to this fear. Even though this is uncommon, the fact that cancer growth can be silent and without symptoms in the early stages may add to the widespread fear of the disease.

Another reason why people find it difficult to regard

cancer as just another disease is the large amount of inaccurate information they receive from the mass media. Sometimes headlines are misleading: for example, RECENT STUDY PREDICTS CANCER CASES IN THE UNITED STATES MAY DOUBLE BY 2030. Just reading the headlines suggests that there will be a cancer epidemic. But reading the article makes it clear that the projected rise in number of cases is based on increased population. More people are living long enough for cancer to develop, and the size of the general population is growing.

Except for lung cancer, the incidence of cancer has not changed much in the last half century, and the chances of an adult's getting cancer are just 30 percent. For children, of course, this percentage is much smaller.

A recent survey by the National Cancer Institute revealed that half of Americans think that "everything causes cancer" and there is not much that can be done to prevent it. Both these ideas are wrong. The cancer epidemic is not the disease itself but fear of the disease. Spreading the word about people who have successfully overcome cancer helps to erase these fears.

Terry is an adolescent cancer survivor. Over a period of several years while she was competing in tennis games, she was also competing in a fight against leukemia. Four years before she was selected for the All-Scholastic team, Terry had her first encounter with cancer. In a tennis tournament at Yale University, Terry suddenly developed severe leg cramps. Because the weather was damp and chilly, doctors blamed the attack on poor playing conditions. But the leg massages and swimming that were supposed to ease the pain did not seem to help. When Terry returned home, medicine stopped the pain in her legs, but she developed cramps in her arms. When her family doctor made some tests, he discovered that her red blood count was low. He referred her to a specialist at Massachusetts General Hospital, where a diagnosis of leukemia was made.

Terry was a thirteen-year-old eighth grader when she

began a program of intensive chemotherapy in which a battery of anticancer drugs were used to attack her disease. Later, her treatment program included a series of radiation treatments and spinal shots to kill any leukemic cells that might be lurking in her brain or spinal cord.

Terry's cancer symptoms disappeared after a month, a condition called remission. However, treatment continued for several years, just in case there were still some cancer cells in her body that might cause a recurrence of the disease. Even though Terry missed fifty days of school that first year, a tutor made it possible for her to finish with a high academic record. And just eight months after her treatment had begun, Terry was able to play tennis again with the approval of her doctor. Although she had to regain her timing and coordination, she was determined to make up for the time she had lost, and she did. Terry became a tennis star in spite of her leukemia, and though not enough time has passed to proclaim a cure, it seems likely that Terry has won her battle against the disease.

Terry's friends were so eager for her return to the tennis courts that they gave little thought to ways of reacting to her illness. But David's seventh-grade classmates were both upset and frightened when they heard he had cancer. Some of them thought they might have cancer too, because they had been so close to him. Unfortunately, these friends did not know that cancer is not contagious.

One boy on the soccer team remembered that David had fallen and hurt his leg shortly before he went to the hospital. There had been pain and swelling in his leg. Did this have anything to do with the tumor? David's whole class had many questions, such as, "What is cancer? What can we say to David if we visit him at the hospital? Will he die?"

David suffered from a form of cancer known as osteosarcoma, the most common type of bone cancer in children and adolescents. Since this form of cancer commonly spreads to other parts of the body, many tests were made to find out whether or not this had happened in

David's case. Fortunately, it had not. But David's leg was removed. He was given an artificial limb.

Long before David returned to school, his classmates took part in a program to learn the facts that are known about cancer. A team of specially trained people helped to make life better for David at home and to prepare his teacher, his classmates, and others at the school for his return. They worked to dispel fears by providing knowledge and understanding of David's disease.

Although much is being done to help young people learn more about cancer and to reduce phobias, many children return to a school where classmates taunt, avoid, and mistreat them in other ways because of their own fear and lack of knowledge.

Although no two cases of cancer are alike, knowing something about cancer will help you feel more comfortable with a person who has cancer. Cancer patients live in a strange world. Learning about it can help you make this world a better place and make your own life more rewarding.

3
What Is Cancer?

Cancer is not just one disease. It is a name for a group of a hundred or more different diseases that have some common characteristics. But all cancers involve cells that reproduce in an abnormal manner.

The process by which they do this is far from simple. Puppies, potatoes, people—all living organisms—are made of cells, small building blocks that can be pictured as tiny spherical balls containing a jelly-like substance called protoplasm. Cells wear out and die at a rate estimated to be several million cells per second in an adult's body. They are being replaced throughout the body all the time, even though we are usually not conscious of the process. However, sometimes the growth of the new cells is obvious.

Suppose you cut your finger. The cells around the gash in your skin receive signals to multiply more rapidly and heal the wound. Then, when healing has taken place, the gash is filled with scar tissue, and the cells receive different signals, which tell them to slow down their rate of division. It may be that, in some cancers, tumor cells multiply by making use of the process that originally evolved to repair wounds.

In most cases, cells grow at a rate that just replaces those that die. There are common instances in which this balance is controlled externally. The growth of nail cells on fingers and toes occurs as new cells push the dead ones ahead. When nails become too long, you file or trim the dead ends away. Hair grows when new hair cells push dead hair cells away from the scalp. In these cases, it is easy to notice cell growth.

If you have ever had a part of your body in a cast, you have probably seen the sheets of dead skin that were shed and had no place to go while the cast was on. When cells can slough off freely, dead skin cells are seldom noticed, except in the case of dandruff and calluses. For example, old skin that remains on your heels may become a problem if its roughness tears stockings. Special kinds of files are made for the removal of these extra cells, and some people find it necessary to rub calluses away with such files almost daily. But for most of the billions of cells in your body, the growing and dying take place without notice.

Embryos are made of cells that grow rapidly. As babies grow to adulthood, the growth rate slows, until there is a steady state, a condition in which the birth of new cells equals the loss of old cells.

Normal cells respond to influences that make them stop growing, but cancer cells do not. One of the greatest mysteries of biology and medicine is the exact reason for this. What gives cells the signal to stop dividing? Scientists do not know. Cancer cells may receive a signal they no longer understand, or they may not receive the normal signal that tells them to stop growing, or the signal may actually be absent.

Even though human cells are so small that it would take a million of them to make a clump the size of the head of a pin, the uncontrolled division of one cell into two and two into four would soon produce a large mass. Suppose cell division continued so that a single cell doubled at the rate of once every 24 hours. In just forty days, there would be enough cells to fill a liter (about a quart). In fifty days, there would be a thousand liters, and in about three months there would be so many cells that they would fill a ball the size of the earth.

Of course, most cancer cells do not divide at this rate. Some cancer cells are sloughed off, and many of them do not divide at all. However, when cancer cells divide, they produce more cancer cells, never normal cells. These cells can pile up to produce a mass of cells known as a solid tumor. There is great variation in the rate at which a tumor doubles in size, but the average doubling time is ninety days. Some tumors double in size in ten days, while others may take as long as four hundred days.

A tumor that doubles its number of cells every six days takes about a month to change from the size of one cell to the size of one centimeter in diameter. A tumor whose doubling time is one hundred days will take eight years to reach the same size. Doubling time is an important factor and one of great concern for cancer patients and their doctors. It is the crowding of normal organs or the outstripping of food supply to them that eventually kills cancer patients.

Mary developed cancer when she was five years old. The tumor was in her brain, and the cells that multiplied to form the tumor interfered with her normal brain function. She had seizures and headaches in the morning, and she vomited frequently.

Before Mary's cancer was diagnosed, her parents could not understand why she always seemed tired and why she ate so poorly. Mary was a child who had always accepted discipline reasonably well, but she was developing serious behavior problems that disrupted the lives of everyone in the family. When Mary's mother and father described these symptoms, the doctors ordered many tests that eventually confirmed their suspicion that Mary was suffering from a brain tumor.

As a group, brain tumors are the second most common cancers of childhood, yet only a very small percentage of children are affected. Many children show symptoms such

22

as Mary's for other reasons. Only medical tests can determine if cancer is involved.

Not all cancers are solid tumors. In fact, the most common form of childhood cancer occurs when cells multiply to form tumors that take on the fluid properties of the organs they affect. About 4 percent of *all* cancers are leukemias, not solid tumors.

Leukemia is characterized by an abnormal number of white blood cells produced by the bone marrow. About 5 percent of all cancers are lymphomas. Although lymphomas may produce solid tumors nearly anyplace in the body, they are characterized by an abnormal number of white blood cells, which in this case are produced by the spleen and lymph nodes. The lymph is a nearly colorless fluid that bathes body cells and moves through a network of vessels and organs known as the lymph nodes, spleen, and thymus gland. These organs produce and store infection-fighting cells, cells of the immune system.

Think of a cell as a factory that is programmed by a computer to produce certain substances. Raw materials are supplied by food from the outside at a rate that is controlled by need. Now think of a cancer cell as a factory whose programming is out of order, causing the continued manufacture of products without taking external needs into account.

In cancer, one might say that the cell is stuck in a dividing phase. Although cancer cells are often thought to be dividing at an unusually fast rate, the lack of cell destruction just makes it seem that way. In fact, many cancer cells divide more slowly than the kinds of cells from which they arose. For example, intestinal cancer cells divide more slowly than normal intestinal cells. However, normal cells in the intestine die off quickly; cancer cells continue to live.

Cancer has been described as a mistake in the division of a single cell. This mistake is programmed into the offspring of the cell, and more errors pile up. The new cells seem to have an advantage over normal cells, allowing them to grow more aggressively.

Cancer cells differ from normal cells in a number of ways. One of these, as we have seen, is the division that piles up cells to form a solid mass or to multiply in the bloodstream at a harmful rate. Another characteristic is the cancer cell's tendency to migrate rather than stay put the way normal cells do. When cancer cells invade other tissues in the body, doctors say the cancer metastasizes.

Think of a cancer that begins as a single cell in the lining of the intestine. This cell divides, and after many divisions some of the cells penetrate the wall of the intestine, and eventually go through it, passing through layers of muscle tissue. Some cancer cells escape into the bloodstream and take up residence in other organs, where they create new tumors. These new tumors will shed cells that also will travel throughout the body and establish themselves in other places. Eventually, the original cancer cell will have a whole host of descendants that monopolize the food supply needed for normal cells.

Sometimes cells divide and form tumors that are not cancerous. These benign tumors are collections of abnormally growing cells that do not spread to other parts of the body. They may be removed surgically and cause no further trouble.

Malignant or bad tumors are those that tend to become progressively worse. In the case of cancer, malignancy implies the ability to invade, to move to other parts of the body and actively destroy normal tissue. Cancerous cells can replace healthy cells. The words "malignant" and "cancer" are sometimes used to describe situations that have no connection with the human body. For example, you might hear someone speak about a cancer or malignancy of some form of society.

Before 1955, scientists did not think that cancers shed cells as soon as they started growing. Now it appears that they do, so probably everyone who has a form of cancer has cancer cells circulating in the bloodstream. It is possible for the immune system to kill some of these cells, when they travel through normal tissue into lymphatic tissue and into the bloodstream. But the immune system can handle only small amounts of such cells, and as a tumor grows it sheds more and more. This is one obvious reason for seeking medical treatment whenever one suspects the presence of cancer.

There is much to be learned before the question "What is cancer?" can be fully answered, but a great deal is already known.

4
Leukemia

Leukemia is the name given to a group of cancers that kill more children between the ages of two and fifteen than any other disease. Although one hears more about leukemia in children than in adults, it is estimated that between five and eight times as many adults are also stricken with this disease. More than half of all cases of leukemia occur in people over sixty years of age. However, the Leukemia Society of America estimates that as many as 25,000 new cases of leukemia are diagnosed in children each year.

The study of cancer continually brings new insights into the care and treatment of victims of leukemia, and researchers look forward to the time when a clear picture of the causes will emerge. There has been dramatic improvement in survival rates for all leukemia patients in recent years, and the leukemia most common in children, acute lymphocytic leukemia (ALL), is considered potentially curable. In spite of great progress, however, 25 percent of young leukemia patients still succumb to the disease.

Leukemia is a malignancy of the blood-forming tissues of the body. The bone marrow, the lymphatic tissues, the spleen, some connective tissues, and some lymph nodes produce immature white blood cells (leukocytes). Leukemia means white blood, a name given to the disease by the German pathologist Rudolf Virchow in 1847, when it was believed to be a malignancy of the blood rather than of the blood-forming tissues.

Leukemia's symptoms are varied. The disease may appear quite suddenly in a child who seems healthy. The mother of three-year-old Sara thought she had a cold, but the cold symptoms did not go away as quickly as they should have. Sara seemed tired and pale, and her appetite was not as good as usual. When Sara had several nosebleeds within a week and complained that her knees hurt inside, her mother took her to see their doctor. The symptoms could indicate anemia, mononucleosis, meningitis, tonsillitis, other kinds of cancer, or other disease, as well as leukemia. The doctor suggested a blood test, but when the blood sample was examined, the evidence was not clear. After a sample of bone marrow tissue was removed from Sara's hip and viewed under the microscope, however, there was no doubt about the diagnosis. The number and nature of the white blood cells showed that Sara had leukemia.

White blood cells play an important part in defending the body against invaders that might cause infection. The two types of white cells most often affected by leukemia are cells that form lymphocytes and granulocytes. By producing antibodies, the lymphocytes combat viruses and bacteria that enter the body. These substances are fatal to infectious organisms. Granulocytes engulf and thus destroy foreign particles that have invaded the body. When they are needed to fight infection, white cells increase rapidly in number; when the infection is over, they are reduced to the normal quantity.

In leukemia, millions of immature and useless white blood cells are produced and the bloodstream is flooded with these useless cells, called "blasts." They accumulate in the blood and in the bone marrow, and eventually the bone marrow is replaced by these abnormal cells. When this happens, the bone marrow cannot produce the normal blood cells that the body needs: blood platelets, red cells, and mature white cells.

Although malignant white blood cells often far outnumber normal white blood cells when a person has leukemia, this is not always the case. No matter what their number, the malignant blood cells circulate through the body and can infiltrate any of the vital organs. The most common form of leukemia in children is the one that affects the lymphocytes, acute lymphocytic leukemia, commonly referred to as ALL. This kind of leukemia, also called lymphoblastic leukemia, accounts for 80 percent of childhood leukemia cases.

Granulocytic leukemia, also known as myelocytic or myelogenous leukemia, is diagnosed in about 18 percent of children with leukemia. Without treatment, 90 percent of acute leukemia victims would die within a year.

The course of sixteen-year-old Robbie De Villiers's leukemia was typical. Robbie, a great baseball fan, was stricken in the summer of 1944. His parents hoped that they could keep him alive until the World Series ended in October, but, as doctors stood helplessly by, Robbie died before the last game was played. In 1949, the De Villiers Foundation, which later became the Leukemia Society of America, was established.

About four years after Robbie De Villiers died, there appeared some small hope for children with leukemia. Dr. Sidney Farber found that a derivative of mustard gas developed during World War II induced the first known remission in childhood leukemia. Although the children in remission died in about eight months, they lived five months longer than expected. The fact that a single drug could slow the course of this disease was considered miraculous. The era of chemotherapy was born.

In the following years, 35,000 chemicals, both natural and synthetic, were screened each year at institutions throughout the United States. The Leukemia Society of America, now active in research for this form of cancer, added its support to the search. Solving the complications of new combinations of drugs was a long agonizing process for researchers, doctors, patients, and their families. Some drugs appeared effective but did not continue to help. Different patients reacted differently to the same drugs or combinations of drugs. Some experimental therapy made patients sicker than they were before they were treated.

Then, in 1967, a major breakthrough in the treatment of ALL in children took place. Doctors realized that treatment should be extended to the patient's central nervous system, for it was here that leukemic cells were escaping the effect of chemotherapy. Irradiation of the brain and spine and injections of antileukemic drugs directly into the spinal fluid were developed at St. Jude's Children's Research Hospital in Memphis, Tennessee, to destroy leukemic cells in the central nervous system. This new therapy proved to be crucial in preventing relapses.

By 1970, doctors were beginning to use the word "cure." The picture was not as bright for children with other types of leukemia, but tremendous progress had been made since 1960, when nearly every leukemic child died within six months.

During the next decade, researchers continued to work toward new treatments for those who could not be cured by chemotherapy. Bone marrow transplants were introduced in the early seventies as a heroic attempt to save those who were dying of leukemia in spite of all the available treatment. Could the patient's diseased bone marrow be regenerated?

One of the problems that delayed the successful use of bone marrow transplants was the need for an identical twin to supply the new marrow. Although investigations into the reasons for rejections of transplants from donors other than identical twins were only beginning, there were some reports of success with siblings. For example, one six-year-old boy with leukemia who had relapsed six times with chemotherapy was operated on with successful results. In the early seventies, an 11 percent cure rate with bone marrow transplantation was considered a triumph, because those patients who lived for a number of years would most certainly have died without them.

The Leukemia Society of America reports today that the overall success rate is rising. Bone marrow transplants are now made while patients are in remission from their leukemia, instead of waiting until they reach the end stages of the disease. In the 1980s, bone marrow transplants mean a possibility of permanent cure for victims of some forms of leukemia.

As in the case of liver and kidney transplants, bone marrow transplants work best when the donor marrow is closely matched to the marrow of the child who receives it. About one third of all leukemia patients have a brother or a sister whose bone marrow can be used in a transplant operation. The chances of finding a matched donor in the general population is believed to be one in ten thousand. But researchers have found ways of overcoming this stumbling block. In one approach, some of the patient's own bone marrow is removed while he or she is in remission. The marrow is banked in a freezer and reimplanted later if it is needed.

In 1979, doctors at Dana-Farber Cancer Institute in Boston announced a new bone marrow transplant for children with leukemia who did not have a suitable family donor. Dr. Robert Bast, one of the doctors who helped to develop this technique, noted that potentially everyone is their own identical twin. If some of the patient's bone marrow could be "cleansed" of leukemia cells, it could be transplanted back to the patient and grow normal cells.

Dr. Jerome Ritz, who worked with Dr. Bast, developed a method of destroying the leukemia cells in the bone marrow before it is returned to the child. In time, the treated bone marrow begins to produce normal, healthy blood components.

During the week that the marrow is being processed, the patient is treated in an isolation room with massive doses of drugs and radiation to destroy any remaining leukemia cells and to protect the child against infection at this time of

30

increased susceptibility. Although bone marrow is removed from the hip bone in the operating room, it can be returned to the patient in the form of a blood transfusion in a vein of the arm. For some reason that is not fully understood, the marrow hones in on the bone cavities and begins to repopulate these areas with normal cells.

Bone marrow transplants are used as an alternative only when drug treatment does not work. As of 1984, about 3,000 bone marrow transplants had been performed in hospitals around the world.

Doctors are very encouraged with their progress both in chemotherapy and bone marrow transplants. They can give real hope to their patients, even to those who have a return of the production of leukemia cells.

A patient in remission may never experience a relapse, a return of the production of leukemia cells and other signs and symptoms of the disease. For most forms of leukemia, a remission that lasts five years after treatment is considered to indicate a cure.

The causes of leukemia are still unknown, but a virus may play a part in some cases. Viruses have been found in some animal leukemias, and they are associated with one kind of human leukemia. Various factors in the environment, such as certain chemicals and radiation, may be involved, especially in adult leukemia. Abnormal genes can play a part too. For example, children with certain birth defects, such as Down's syndrome or a severe form of anemia, seem to be at increased risk of developing leukemia. It is widely believed that all these factors alter the genetic makeup of leukemic cells, allowing them to escape from the normal functioning of body tissues.

Much progress has been made over the last fifteen years in the understanding and control of leukemia. The sense of hope is especially great for child sufferers, as illustrated by the slogan of the Leukemia Society of America: COUNT-DOWN TO CURE . . . IT'S A MATTER OF TIME.

5

Other Kinds of Cancer in the Young

Bone Cancer

Bone cancers are most commonly found in children and young adults, principally between the ages of ten and twenty. They account for about 5 percent of childhood cancers. The incidence of osteosarcoma (osteogenic sarcoma) peaks in late adolescence, after a period of rapid bone growth, and is more common in boys than in girls.

There are many theories about the causes of bone cancer, but none has been proved. Since some forms of bone cancer are more common in young people who are significantly taller than average, it has been suggested that increased production of a growth factor, as yet unidentified, may be a cause. However, the annual incidence of bone cancer in the ten-to-twenty age group is only 1 out of 100,000, so a very small proportion of young people are affected.

The bones most frequently involved are the large bones of the upper arm (humerus) and the leg (femur and tibia) and the weight-bearing pelvic bones. The most common symptom is pain. At first this pain may occur only at night, or it may be worse at night than in the day. The pain may be constant or it may only occur from time to time. In some cases it is relieved by exercise, but sometimes just the opposite is true, making a patient favor an arm or a leg that is not involved. The second most common symptom is swelling, owing to the growth of the tumor.

When Paul complained of pains in his leg, his family wondered if the teenager had arthritis. Even his doctor was not certain about the cause of the pain. After Paul's leg was X-rayed, the doctor suspected osteosarcoma from the way the bone appeared on the X-ray films, but still he was not certain. The doctor explained to Paul and his parents that the disease he suspected was often confused with arthritis, local infection, effects of injury, glandular deficiency, vitamin deficiency, and benign tumors. A biopsy to remove tissue that could be examined under the microscope was the only certain way to check the diagnosis.

When Paul first learned that he had cancer, he felt he was dreaming. Cancer was something that happened to other people; it could never happen to him. Since the chances of a young person's ever having any kind of cancer are slight, Paul's feelings were not unusual or unrealistic.

For a few days, Paul was convinced that he was not going to live much longer. He did not want to hear what could be done for him until several days after he first heard the news that he had developed cancer. Then he calmed down and talked with a doctor at the hospital, with some nurses, and with a social worker. He felt a lot different about himself when he got used to the idea that he had cancer. He even began making plans for the ways he would manage if his leg had to be removed.

Treatment for Paul's kind of cancer involved surgery to remove the affected leg and a course of chemotherapy using one or more of the anticancer drugs. His artificial limb and physical rehabilitation were important parts of his therapy.

Paul found that he had to find new ways of doing hundreds of things that make up everyday life. He worked hard to learn how to swim and ride his bike again. But today, six years after his cancer was discovered, he is living a normal and productive life as a salesman for a pharmaceutical firm. In his free time, Paul goes back to the hospital where he was treated to talk to children who have just learned that they have cancer. He makes friends with them, shows the osteosarcoma patients how well he can walk, and brings in pictures of himself on his bicycle. His volunteer work fills the lives of many children with hope.

The outlook for patients with osteosarcoma has improved within the last eight years. Treatment may still consist of removing the affected extremity and following this with chemotherapy for a year or so after the surgery. However, some young people with bone cancer are being treated successfully by the removal of bone sections rather than amputation. Doctors are constantly working toward limb-saving procedures with new surgical techniques.

Ewing's sarcoma, or Ewing's tumor, differs from osteosarcoma in that it affects a different part of the bone, beginning with the marrow in the bone cavity. It can occur in almost any bone in the body and frequently spreads to the lungs, other bones, the lymph nodes, and the central nervous system before it is diagnosed. Like osteosarcoma, it tends to occur in children and young people between the ages of ten and twenty.

Although the symptoms of Ewing's sarcoma—fever, pain, and weakness—are different from those of osteosarcoma, they are also common to a number of other diseases. A true diagnosis depends on a biopsy. If the biopsy is positive, a bone survey, bone scans, chest X-ray films, and liver, lung, and brain tests are made to determine whether the disease has spread.

Ewing's sarcoma accounts for about one third of the cases of bone cancer in white children in the United States. It is rare in black children anywhere, a fact that leads some doctors to suspect that a genetic factor may be involved.

A great deal of progress has been made in controlling the tumor in the place where the disease begins, because Ewing's sarcoma is very sensitive to radiation therapy. Usually the primary tumor can be eliminated by irradiation alone, but sometimes surgery is involved. This is especially true for cancers of the rib bones. Chemotherapy has improved the results of both surgery and radiation in controlling the primary tumor.

More research is under way to determine the best combination of treatments for children whose disease has spread to other organs. It is hoped that such treatments will lead to improved life spans.

Brain Tumor

Brain tumors, as a group, are the second most common type of childhood cancer (after leukemia). Although they tend to occur in the first ten years of life, they are sometimes seen in adolescents.

When two-year-old Kathy woke each morning, she fussed because her head hurt, but she could not really explain that she had a headache. Most children do not normally experience headaches, so this was an important symptom that would help the doctor diagnose her problem. Kathy's parents were not alerted by her clumsiness, which they attributed to the poor coordination of a two-year-old. But when Kathy vomited several mornings before breakfast and then asked for food, they were confused and concerned.

After many tests, Kathy's tumor was surgically removed, and in her particular case there was a good chance that she would recover. Surgery was followed by radiation treatments, and Kathy was given anticancer drugs intravenously that would penetrate the brain and the central nervous system. Her parents were warned to watch for symptoms that might mean a recurrence of her cancer.

The outlook for children who develop malignant brain tumors is cloudy. Much depends on the individual case. While researchers continue to explore the nature of brain tumors, a team of caregivers works with the patients and their families.

Lymphoma

Lymphoma is the name given to a group of malignant disorders that affect lymphatic tissues. The lymph system is a network of tiny vessels connecting hundreds of bean-sized glands, or nodes. A clear fluid, composed mostly of the type of white blood cells known as lymphocytes, circulates through the system. In addition to the lymph nodes, the system includes the spleen, thymus, and certain parts of other organs, such as the tonsils, stomach, small intestine, and skin.

The type of lymphoma differs with the kind of cell that is affected. Hodgkin's disease, the most common, tends to involve lymph nodes near the surface of the body. It accounts for about half of childhood lymphomas and about 6 percent of all childhood cancers and occurs most often in young adults. The survival rate is 75 to 95 percent.

The most common early sign of Hodgkin's disease is a swelling of the lymph glands, usually on either side of the neck but sometimes in the armpits or groin. Medical tests are usually made only after glands have been swollen for several weeks, because many infections can also cause lymph glands to swell.

Both Hodgkin's and non-Hodgkin's lymphomas occasionally cluster in families and are more common in boys than in girls. Like leukemia, some cases seem linked with rare, genetically determined immune-system diseases.

Non-Hodgkin's lymphomas tend to develop in the bowel and in the midsection of the chest. As the disease progresses, it spreads through the lymph system to other parts of the body. Early symptoms may include swelling of the abdomen, face, or neck and difficulty in swallowing or in breathing.

Except in the case of Hodgkin's disease, most lymphomas in young people seem to be spread throughout the body even though tumors appear in just one region. Chemotherapy, which reaches throughout the body, is the usual form of treatment. St. Jude's Children's Research Hospital reports that new treatment approaches result in high survival rates in certain cases.

Neuroblastoma

Neuroblastoma is a cancer that develops in young nerve cells. More than half of these tumors occur in the adrenal glands, located in the abdominal area near the kidneys. An enlarging abdomen with a mass is a common sign.

Neuroblastoma, though not found in adults, is the most common solid tumor in children. One fourth of the children who suffer from this disease show some symptoms in the first year of life and the remainder do so before the age of five. The disease accounts for about 8 percent of childhood tumors in children under fifteen, but the total number of cases is only 7 to 20 per million births. The cancer in as many as 70 percent of these children will have spread to various parts of the body by the time the disease is diagnosed.

Treatment consists of surgery to remove as much of the cancerous growth as possible. It may be followed by radiation, chemotherapy, or both. Despite treatment, the two-year survival rate for children with widespread neuroblastoma is about 5 percent. Infants whose primary tumors develop at a site other than the adrenals and whose disease is limited when it is diagnosed have a much better chance. A new treatment program has been developed at St. Jude's Children's Research Hospital. As a result, more than half the children with neuroblastoma that has spread achieve complete remission.

Retinoblastoma

Retinoblastoma is a rare eye disease in which a malignant tumor forms on the retina. About 60 percent of all cases are not hereditary and affect one eye; about 15 percent are hereditary and affect one eye, and about 25 percent are hereditary and affect both eyes. About 5 percent of the people who carry this gene do not develop the tumor.

In many cases, the symptoms of retinoblastoma are first noticed in babyhood, with seventeen months the average age of diagnosis. The earliest evidence of the tumor is a white reflex known as cat's-eye reflex or white pupil. It is best seen under a bright light when the child looks forward. Sometimes parents bring the symptoms to the doctor's attention by saying that the child has a strange expression. Some ask the doctor to look at the glow in their child's eye.

If diagnosis is made early, the tumor may be destroyed by irradiation and normal vision preserved. If the tumor is large, the affected eye may be removed, but if both eyes are involved, every effort is made to preserve vision in at least one eye. If the tumor is very small, a laser beam may be used to combat it. In some cases, freezing and thawing the tumor several times destroys the major circulation to the tumor and the tumor cells themselves. Chemotherapy, irradiation, or both may be used to treat a child in which the cancer has spread to other parts of the body.

The removal of an eye in a very young child is difficult for both the patient and the parents. Some parents find it extremely helpful to meet other children who have undergone surgery for retinoblastoma. Seeing young children with artificial eyes who are healthy, active, and attractive can be a tremendous source of comfort to them and, in turn, makes things easier for the child.

Rhabdomyosarcoma (Rhabdosarcoma)

Rhabdomyosarcoma is a disease of the muscle cells, a form of childhood cancer in which the symptoms are easily recognizable. The presence of a noticeable lump usually alerts parents to seek treatment for children in the early stages of the disease, so that even though rhabdomyosarcoma usually grows and spreads rapidly, treatment can be started early.

The early symptoms depend on the location of the tumor. One in the throat may cause hoarseness or difficulty in swallowing. One near the eye may lead to a vision problem. The tumor usually is found in the head and neck area, the pelvis, or the extremities, but since it originates in the muscle tissue, it may be found almost anywhere.

There are two distinct age peaks for rhabdomyosarcoma: one before age five and the other in the teens. There is some suspicion that cancers of the early age group form before birth.

Treatment involves surgery, irradiation, and chemotherapy, but if the tumor is so large that surgery may be dangerous for the patient, the tumor may be reduced in size by irradiation, chemotherapy, or both before surgery. Sometimes irradiation and chemotherapy are the only treatments. Although patients with tumors in some areas do poorly, much progress has been made in the treatment of rhabdomyosarcoma. The two-year survival rate is now about 70 percent, compared to only 20 percent in the early 1960s.

Wilms' Tumor

Wilms' tumor is a cancer that begins in the cells of the kidney. Almost without exception, this cancer is found in children ranging from infancy to the age of fifteen. It is quite different from the kind of cancer found in adult kidneys. Scientists think Wilms' tumor starts in immature cells that would normally become mature kidney cells.

The kidneys are a matched pair of organs located on either side of the backbone below the liver and the stomach. They are necessary for life because they remove wastes from the body by making urine. Kidneys filter urea (the main waste material in urine), salt, and other substances from the blood as it flows through them.

Wilms' tumor is the fifth most common kind of childhood cancer, but only about 350 cases of it are reported in the United States each year, and most of them occur in children under five years of age. There are no unique symptoms for this disease. Parents are often the first to discover the tumor when they notice a hard mass in a small child's abdomen after bathing or while dressing. Blood in the urine can be a sign of Wilms' tumor, but it can also be a sign of other disorders. Most of the time, blood in the urine in the case of Wilms' tumor is so slight that it is visible only when viewed through a microscope. Symptoms such as loss of appetite, loss of weight, fever, fatigue, and anemia may also be present, as they are in other types of cancer.

There are a few children who are more apt to develop Wilms' tumor than others. For example, when the colored portion of the eye, the iris, is absent, a child has a condition known as aniridia. In about 1 in 173 cases of Wilms' tumor, aniridia is present, compared with 1 out of 50,000 cases in the overall population. Children who have aniridia consistently lack a segment of chromosome number 13. Scientists have found it especially interesting that one set of twins lacked both an iris and the chromosome segment, but only one twin developed Wilms' tumor. This finding led support to the idea that the predisposition to cancer is inherited, but that some second event is needed for the cancer to develop.

An enlargement of a part of the body or abnormal development of the genitals or urinary tract is frequently associated with Wilms' tumor.

About eight out of ten children who suffer from Wilms' tumor can be expected to live for many years without its recurrence. Although doctors hesitate to say that they can cure this form of cancer, what can happen seems to be the equivalent of a cure.

Wilms' tumor is one of about twenty cancers for which treatments have been developed that combine surgery, radiation therapy, and chemotherapy. The way in which these treatments are used depends on the individual child's general health, age, and other factors. Surgery was not part of the treatment for children under the age of two until recent years, when advances in surgical techniques and medical care made it possible. Radiation therapy is not often used on children under the age of two, but chemotherapy is used to treat just about all cases of Wilms' tumor.

6
Tests and Treatments

There is no universally accepted definition of cancer. Estimates of the number of different kinds range from one hundred to almost three hundred, yet many of the same tests and treatments are used for all cancer patients. Here is a brief description of some of these tests and treatments.

Test Procedures

A **biopsy** is a microscopic examination of tumor tissue. This test determines whether or not a tumor is malignant and, if it is, what kind of cancer is present. A general anesthesia may be used because of the location of a tumor. In some cases, local anesthesia is all that is necessary. A frozen section may be made during surgery for a preliminary opinion, but the specimen is taken from the tissue and prepared in a different way for further study by the pathologist, a physician trained to identify changes in body cells caused by disease.

Blood studies include a variety of tests. Blood may be drawn in a syringe from a vein in the arm or obtained by a finger stick, in which a small prick is made in a finger and a few drops of blood are squeezed out. A white blood count (WBC) is a common procedure in evaluating the blood of

41

young people who are suspected of or have been diagnosed as having cancer. The number of white cells per cubic millimeter of blood in healthy people has been established, and the patient's number of white cells is compared with this. Patients receiving chemotherapy, drugs to fight cancer, usually have a lower-than-normal white cell count. Leukemic patients have a higher-than-average count. This test is used to detect the presence of leukemic blasts.

Hemoglobin is measured to determine the amount of this substance in the red blood cells that carry oxygen. Lower-than-normal hemoglobin counts may mean the patient is anemic. Sometimes a sudden appearance of anemia is associated with a return of cancer cells in the body. Anemia is also one of the common side effects of chemotherapy.

Hematocrit is a measure of the amount of red blood cells.

Platelets are a part of the blood involved in stopping bleeding. If the number of platelets is low, more tests are made to find out why.

Normal values for complete blood counts are:
   Hemoglobin: 9.6 to 15
   Platelets: 150,000 to 300,000
   White cells: 4,500 to 10,000

Blood marrow aspiration is a procedure used to find out whether or not there are cancer cells in bone marrow. The patient is usually asked to lie face down with a pillow under the pelvis. After the skin is numbed with a local anesthetic, a long needle is inserted to draw the marrow into a syringe. The procedure lasts only about five or ten minutes, but it can be stressful and may cause pain. Many times, patients are helped to relax so that the procedure is less painful.

Bone marrow biopsy is a procedure that provides doctors with a larger amount of bone marrow than can be obtained by aspiration. It is somewhat similar but more painful. Bone marrow may be taken from each hip bone.

Computerized axial tomography (CAT scan) is a relatively new test in which X-rays are used to detect masses in the body. The child or young person is told to lie still while a narrow X-ray beam is directed by computer to revolve around him or her. Thousands of bits of information are registered in less than a minute, and these are translated by computer into a cross-section picture on a viewing screen. A printout is made so that doctors can refer to the information for future detailed analysis.

Lumbar puncture, or **spinal tap,** is used for several reasons. Some cancers tend to spread to the spinal cord or to the covering of the brain, and if this has happened, cancer cells will be found in the fluid that surrounds the brain and spinal cord. Lumbar punctures, or spinal taps, are also used as a means of administering medicine directly to the brain and spinal cord during chemotherapy and as a way to look for infection.

The child or young person is asked to lie on one side and pull the legs up so that the body is in as tight a ball as possible with the backbone projecting backward. A local anesthetic is applied to the lower back and a needle is inserted into the fluid space between the vertebrae and the spinal cord. A sample of this fluid is collected and examined for cancer cells and other materials. After the fluid is collected, medicines may be given through the puncture.

Headaches are not uncommon after lumbar punctures, and nausea and vomiting may follow the injection of anticancer drugs. Although the test itself takes only about five or ten minutes, getting the patient to relax before the test is important.

Scans are used to discover tumors in organs such as the brain, bones, liver, and kidneys. Chemicals that collect in certain organs are made radioactive and either swallowed or injected. After a certain waiting period, which gives the chemical time to collect in the organ in question, electronic devices are used to track the material and special cameras called scanners take pictures. This enables doctors to tell whether or not organs are functioning properly and whether or not they contain abnormal masses, or tumors. Except for the injection of the radioactive chemical, these tests are painless.

Ultrasound studies, called sonograms, make pictures through the use of sound waves. The patient lies on a table and a small instrument that emits sound waves is passed across the body several times. Sounds waves that are too high to be heard by human ears bounce off, creating an echo pattern. Since tumors generate different echoes from normal tissues, ultrasound can distinguish masses that are cancerous from those that are not. The sound waves can be changed electronically into images, so that doctors can study the pictures at their leisure.

X-rays of various parts of the body are used to examine specific organs where symptoms give doctors reason to suspect some abnormality. Various chemicals are used to make organs more visible. For example, in an arteriogram, an X-ray picture of the arteries, capillaries, and veins, dye is injected into an artery in the groin. The blood vessels will then show up in the X-ray films that are taken as the dye travels in the blood. This procedure can detect any tumors that are pressing on the blood vessels or in the vessels themselves. It can also show the blood supply to a tumor.

Treatment Programs

Treatment programs are individual, but they are based on medical advances learned from treating many other young patients. Most patients receive surgery, radiation therapy, or chemotherapy or a combination of these. All treatment aims to bring about a decrease or disappearance of the cancer.

When the symptoms of cancer have decreased or disappeared, a person is said to be in remission. The first treatment attempts to bring about a remission. After this, therapy is continued in an effort to eliminate the cancer. Doctors call these two phases of treatment "remission induction" and "remission maintenance." Remission induction may involve surgery, chemotherapy, and irradiation. Remission maintenance involves chemotherapy that may range in time from a few months to many years.

Surgery is almost always the primary treatment for solid tumors. If a tumor is very large, irradiation and chemotherapy may first be used to reduce the size of the tumor. This makes the operation safer and lessens physical and functional defects.

Chemotherapy is the treatment of cancer with drugs, which may be administered by mouth or by injection into a muscle, a vein, or just below the skin. Getting the drugs into the bloodstream spreads them throughout the body. With brain tumors and in the prevention of central nervous system disease in leukemia, drugs are injected into the spinal fluid.

Anticancer drugs interfere with the duplication and growth of cancer cells by depriving them of a substance they need to function or by preventing their division, or both, so the cells are eventually destroyed. Unfortunately, anticancer drugs also affect other rapidly dividing normal cells such as those in the digestive system, bone marrow, hair follicles, and reproductive system. For this reason, side effects often occur, although this is not true in all cases. Almost all side effects are temporary, but they can be very upsetting to the patient.

Some side effects of chemotherapy occur immediately. Pain at the injection site may be accompanied by an uncomfortable burning sensation. If the drug leaks from the vein during the IV (intravenous procedure), it may severely burn the skin. Care must be taken to see that the needle is securely in place while the drug is being administered.

Nausea and vomiting are frequent side effects that vary in intensity. One patient recalled eight hours of vomiting but referred to that time as eight hours that saved his life. Although many young patients can relate the unpleasant side effects to the benefit of the drugs, little children cannot. Less common immediate side effects include hives, rashes, swelling of eyelids, hands, and feet, and shortness of breath. Some drugs cause constipation or diarrhea.

Common delayed side effects include loss of hair, mouth sores, and ulcers. Certain drugs, such as the prednisone common in leukemia chemotherapy, cause a child to gain weight. Hair loss and weight gain often have a greater emotional effect on young people than the concern of having cancer.

Immunotherapy is based on the theory that a cancer patient's body can be strengthened so as to destroy the cancer cells. Immune therapies attempt to stimulate the immune system, a complex network that fights substances foreign to the body. Many different approaches are being studied in efforts to combat cancer through immune therapies. Some of these that have already met rigorous criteria are recognized by medical centers, while others are highly controversial.

Irradiation is frequently used to destroy cancer cells and reduce the size of a tumor through the use of X-rays, radium, or other sources of ionizing radiation. This destroys the genetic code within the cells that directs development, causing the cells to die as they are about to divide. Care is taken to prevent the exposure of healthy tissue by the use of special shields made of lead through which the rays cannot pass. Insofar as possible, the doses used to kill the cancer cells have a minimal effect on the surrounding tissue.

Sometimes, parents or children fear that they will be radioactive after radiation treatment. This is not the case. However, there may be some side effects, such as hair loss, in the area receiving the radiation. If the radiation treatment is aimed at the abdominal area, there may be nausea, vomiting, and diarrhea. If the target is the neck or head, the patient may suffer from a dry and sore mouth, with loss of appetite. Skin damage in the treated area may cause itching, pain, and extra sensitivity to sunlight.

Nutrition is a special problem for children with cancer. Eating hints, special diets, recipes, and tips for eating and related problems can be obtained without cost from the National Cancer Institute. See Further Information, at the back of the book.

7

Young Cancer Patients Speak Out

Children who suffer from cancer live in a strange world from the time they learn of their diagnosis. Many will undergo a long series of unpleasant treatments before they return home and go back to school. Some may never return home or live even till their next birthday, or more than a few years. Some will be in remission for a period of time, only to learn that they must once more go through a long series of difficult treatments.

An increasingly large number of young people live a long time after their cancers have first been diagnosed. A new and better understanding is growing of the emotional needs of these patients, their families, and others with whom they come in contact. Some of this understanding has come from the observations of the youngsters themselves.

How do children face the possibility of death? How do they react to pain? What can be done to make each day count? These are questions to which many children have given answers.

For example, ten-year-old Matthew Lancaster lived with Ewing's sarcoma for a year and a half. He described his world in an illustrated book dedicated to all people who have cancer titled *Hang Toughf*. Along with his description of being scared, of the pain and unpleasantness of the treatments, this ten-year-old offers advice for people of all ages. He assures others that they can grit their teeth and bear it and that they are not alone in the unfair situation of having developed cancer. He tells of the importance of a positive attitude; the need to keep telling yourself you can do it. Along with his childlike pictures of an ugly night nurse, a mad doctor who is going to give him a shot, and a beach with bright sunshine that he pictures when he gets ready for a blood test, Michael includes positive messages for cancer patients of all ages.

A group of children facing life-and-death situations at the Center for Attitudinal Healing shared their experiences with terminal illness and the way they helped each other cope with the physical and emotional pain in a paperback book titled *There Is a Rainbow Behind Every Dark Cloud*. Most of these children were between the ages of eight and thirteen, although volunteers and professionals worked with the group. Their philosophy is based on *A Course in Miracles*, published by the Foundation for Inner Peace, in New York City. Basically, the group believes that healing takes place when they feel nothing but love and when they are no longer frightened or feeling bad about anything. After telling what they have experienced, they devote a part of the book to "choices you have in helping yourself." Many children learned that they could be happy "inside" even though they did not like what was happening outside.

Other children who have been victims of cancer have spoken out in letters to families, to other children, to hospital newspapers and in organization newsletters such as the Candlelighters Childhood Cancer Foundation *Youth Newsletter*. The Candlelighters organization was formed in 1970, in Washington, D.C., California, and Florida, by groups of parents who met to discuss their mutual problems. Today, they are organized as a foundation that includes 218 groups throughout the world. The 17,000 people on their national mailing list include parents and medical professionals who treat children with cancer. The newsletter is one of their many contributions to those interested in the cancer problem. It is supported by tax-exempt donations and a grant from the American Cancer Society.

The Candlelighters *Youth Newsletter* provides information to young cancer patients and others. With its news for young patients on how their peers are surviving, coping, and enjoying life to the fullest, it is a positive outlet for young people living with cancer.

Here is a poem that a fourteen-year-old girl wrote for the newsletter a year and a half after losing one leg above the knee because of osteogenic sarcoma. She underwent chemotherapy for a year and was in remission when the poem was written. She plans to be a doctor and "maybe help other children who have cancer."

PLEASE DON'T STARE
By Marne Beckmeyer

Sometimes life is hard to bear,
  Because the people, they all stare.

They smile a frightened smile and go,
  But deep inside I want to know.

Are the people scared of me?
  Or are they scared of what they see?

Even though I have one leg, not two,
  I can do the same things as you.

My appearance is different,
  But inside I'm the same,
  So please stop this staring game.

Marne has no complaints about her friends. She says they don't stare at her, but strangers look, then look away. When children ask her what happened to her, Marne would rather tell them than have their mothers pull the children away before she can answer. A poster person for fund raising for a Variety Club effort to raise money for a pediatric cancer center at Johns Hopkins in Baltimore, Marne is speaking out to others in many ways.

A number of children wrote and drew about their thoughts, feelings, and experiences in a small book called *What Happened to You Happened to Me*. Each section in this book deals with experiences that so many young people who have cancer have in common. They tell how they felt about their diagnosis, hospital experiences, surgery, irradiation, clinic visits, hair loss, side effects, return to school, activities, feelings, and experiences, and they describe how they have changed.

Each child's experience with cancer is different, depending on the kind of cancer, the stage of the cancer, the age of the child, the hospital staff, and other factors. Feelings when they first learn about cancer range widely, since some children know more about the seriousness of the disease than others. Many children feel frightened, mad, upset, and worried. "Why has this happened to *me*?" is a very normal reaction.

The very young child struggles with fears of separation, abandonment, and loneliness when placed in a hospital setting. There are strange faces, strange happenings, in the absence of familiar and cherished toys and family members. Along with the terror of separation from family comes an anger that the all-powerful parents cannot or will not prevent treatments that are often unpleasant, painful, and sometimes disfiguring. Children respond differently, but many express their anxiety and hostility either through violent outbursts or silence and withdrawal. Some children cry and cling to parents, eat and sleep poorly, and respond with anger even to the friendliest approaches. Many children respond best to friendly overtures from another child.

Beginning with age five or six, children have fears relating to physical and bodily harm. The Leukemia Society of America reports that children between five and ten sense

50

when they are seriously ill, in spite of efforts to keep them from being aware of this.

Children over ten speak of their fear of death and seem to become especially worried when confronted with a conspiracy of silence. When they can speak out about their concerns with a sympathetic adult, they show signs of relief.

In an effort to protect their parents, some young children avoid speaking out about their anxieties or their own awareness of their condition. Such a case is cited in *Emotional Aspects of Leukemia*. Lucy, a six-year-old whose parents felt certain they had succeeded in keeping knowledge of the seriousness of her illness from their daughter, was interviewed by a psychologist. When asked to draw a picture and tell a story about what was happening in it, Lucy drew what she described as a little girl in a hospital bed. The little girl was pretending to be asleep, according to Lucy, so her mommy would not know that she had heard the doctor describe how sick her child is. Knowing would make the mommy cry.

Other children speak through pictures of the way they feel about treatments. One drew a hypodermic needle with a hook on the end and labeled it a fishhook. Another drew four monsters and labeled them nurse, doctor, mom and dad. This was his way of expressing his feeling that his parents should not be permitting the unpleasant treatment he was getting.

Many children who suffer from cancer are allowed to express their feelings through art, puppets, and reactions to toys. One boy always pounded the doctor doll in the playroom as soon as he arrived. Then he would go about his normal play.

Many older children express their anger verbally by scolding nurses, doctors, parents, or anyone else who happens to be there. They feel that parents have let them down because they are unable to prevent the treatments or the illness itself. Children who would like to express anger at those who administer treatments are fearful of doing so. They may let it out when parents are with them alone. This is hard for many parents to understand without the help of social workers and other professionals.

Adolescent cancer patients have a particularly difficult time, for they are living through a period of wanting to express independence at a time when parents feel the need to be overprotective. The disease forces the teenager to be dependent on caregivers and may increase the need to rebel against authority figures. One teenager expressed the feeling that his mother was taking over his life. Sometimes she acted as if he were two years old and other times as if he were ninety-two and couldn't do anything for himself.

One of the side effects of treatment about which young cancer patients are most vocal is hair loss. Attitudes range from knowing that they can get some new hair but cannot get a new life, to feeling so terrible about it that they cry constantly. One girl complained that wigs itched, felt hot, and looked artificial. She wore a hat all the time, but she always had the feeling that someone would run up behind her and pull the hat off.

After a time, children may be able to joke about their bald heads. One boy said bald was beautiful because he could get his scalp so clean when he took a shower. Some sew false hair on their scarves to make bangs. Children may realize that anyone who makes fun of a head that is bald from cancer treatment does so because he or she is scared. Some patients say that if your friends tease you, they aren't your friends, while others join in good-natured teasing. One girl who lost her wig while playing ball laughed about it, and then the others who were playing the game laughed too. She described it as a funny situation that didn't hurt anybody.

One of the problems expressed by young cancer patients is not knowing what to say when people ask questions. Some good answers came from talking to other young people in the hospital who had been there a long time or who had been there before. One of the things they empha-sized was for each of them to remember that, even though things changed on the outside, they were still themselves inside. And they emphasized the need to hope.

8

Camps and Other Fun
for Young Cancer Patients

Children with cancer are normal children with
special problems, according to Dr. Edward S. Baum of
Children's Memorial Hospital in Chicago, Illinois. Dr.
Baum heads a recently formed national volunteer organization, Children's Oncology Camps of America. Beginning
with a camp here and a camp there, the number has grown
so that there are about fifty in various parts of the United
States.

Children with cancer are not admitted to many camps for
healthy children. Their disease and the treatments have
dominated and limited their lives, and thousands of them
have watched brothers, sisters, and friends go off to a
summer of fun.

Today, there are many camps that admit only children
with cancer and, in some cases, their brothers and sisters.
Cancer camps are open to any child with cancer, whether in
remission, undergoing therapy, cured, or at a stage where
no further therapy can help. All that is required is that the
child is well enough to have a reasonable chance to enjoy
the experience of some normal camp activities.

The number of camps continues to grow, perhaps because they are so rewarding, both for the campers and the
staff. Counselors include mothers, fathers, brothers, or sis-

ters of patients, older patients themselves, medical personnel, and other interested persons who offer their services. When Gary Mervis founded Camp Good Days in Pittsford, New York, there were 450 applicants for the camp's 85 counselor jobs, including attorneys, recreation specialists, a judge, a TV specialist who was covering the story, and others.

Volunteers at cancer camps often use their summer vacation time to work there, and they, along with the doctors, nurses, and medical technicians, take no money. However, even though staff services are free and campsites are usually donated, the cost of running such a camp is far more than the campers pay. Private donations and grants from the American Cancer Society and other organizations make them possible. In some cases, large grants help to increase the amount of time camps can stay open. Camp Ronald McDonald for Good Times may be open year round to accommodate hundreds of children in the Los Angeles area with cancer.

Each camp for children with cancer has a medical station complete with the full-time services of a doctor, nurse, and medical technician. Most of the day's schedule resembles that of other camps, with hiking, fishing, horseback riding, canoeing and swimming, as well as storytelling and singing around the evening campfire. During their busy schedules, campers take time out for visits to the "Med Shed," where they get medication by shots or IV drips or have tubes that are implanted in their chests cleaned so that medication can flow freely into their bodies. Most children with cancer take their medication at mealtime quite regularly and report to the medical tents voluntarily, for they know the importance of their treatments. Getting children to cooperate with medication is not a major problem. Dr. Baum reports that the most common problems at the One Step at a Time Camp are the same as those seen at any summer camp: athletic bruises, homesickness, personality clashes, and complaints about food.

The volunteers who staff the camps for young cancer

patients report that they get something more valuable than money for their efforts. The courage of the children and the joy that camp brings to them are rewarding. Sometimes, parents report changes that camp has made. For example, one mother wrote that her son always wore a baseball cap to hide his baldness, but he came home from camp with a sunburned head. Another boy, who had refused to go outside after his leg was amputated, became the best roller skater at the camp. A child who had become so withdrawn that she would not speak to anyone started to talk at camp and continued talking when she returned home. One volunteer reported that everyone gains at camp. He remarked, "For the children, camp is one of the few immediate and tangible experiences they live for. For the volunteers, the satisfactions are as immediate and tangible as you could ever experience." One doctor reported that he really believed some terminally ill children stay alive just for camp.

Whether they go to Camp Sky High Hope, Camp Can-Do, Camp Bet'U Can, Camp Rainbow, Camp Sunshine, or any other camp for children with cancer, most campers make friends and have a wonderful time. This fulfills an important goal of treatment programs concerned with the emotional welfare of patients as well as their physical condition.

A visitor to a cancer camp might see some unusual and inspiring sights. At Camp One Step at a Time, a thirteen-year-old whose leg has been amputated learns to climb a stone wall by hopping to the first step and using his arms to raise himself to the place where his one remaining leg can reach a higher place. He is learning rock climbing, a sport that most adults have never tried. Another boy tosses his itchy wig in his backpack as he hikes through the woods. A girl leaves her artificial leg on the dock when she dives in the water. These are just a few experiences almost taken for granted by the more than 200 children who are attending this camp in one summer. Many of the campers plan to return next year. A few of them may die before camp opens again, a situation that most campers accept realistically. In some camps, a tree is planted in memory of each child who dies.

Cancer camp is not a sad place. Even children who know they will not live long enjoy themselves. As one girl remarked, "They tell me I am going to die soon, but I want to have fun as long as I can."

Not every child expects the cancer camp to be fun. For example, Todd really didn't like the idea of going to camp last summer, especially since he had not been feeling well. After he learned that his cancer was under control, he felt like getting away from everything connected with the disease. The long months of treatment made him feel that cancer was everywhere. If he could just spend the summer at home, perhaps things would be the way they used to be.

Of course, he would still have to go to the hospital for tests. Of course, his friends would still know that he had cancer and treat him differently. Of course, his parents would still try to overprotect him the way they had since they learned of his cancer. But go away to camp? He had never wanted to go to camp in the first place. What would a cancer camp be like?

Mr. Bruce had presented a slide show at the Medical Center Hospital for nurses, doctors, social workers, parents of children with cancer, and the children themselves. Todd admitted that some of the activities sounded good. He had never been on a horse. He had never even dreamed about going up in a hot-air balloon. Some of the other activities did not sound too different from what he did every summer. He could swim in the lake, go canoeing, and hike in the mountains without spending a single night away from home.

Todd's parents seemed to have made up their minds about his going to camp. Mr. Bruce's arguments had been very convincing. There was medical care at the camp. The campers would be treated just like any other person in their age group, even though each camper was a cancer patient. So Todd was one of about twenty young people who were stuffed into the bus with other new campers. No one seemed to want to go except for one youngster named Bob. He had been there the year before, and he thought the camp was great.

Todd soon made friends at the camp. He was especially glad about this, for he felt that some of his friends at home had been avoiding him since they learned of his disease. He knew that he had alienated some of his old friends because he did not want to take the chance of having them feel sorry for him or do things for him just because he was sick. Going to camp where every other boy and girl had cancer had some advantages, Todd decided. He was treated like a normal person, even though he was bald and had to have his blood count checked periodically. Todd was not the only one who had lost all his hair from radiation treatments. He was not the only one who had experienced the nausea that followed chemotherapy, the drug treatments aimed at killing the cancer cells that made him feel miserable.

In spite of all their problems, the campers could laugh at themselves. When they were drenched with rain on a hike, someone remarked that the only thing worse than having long wet hair was having a wet head with no hair. When they saw a squirrel without much hair on its tail, they said the squirrel must have had chemotherapy.

The campers could talk about how it hurt when the nurse could not find a vein, how they worried about the cancer coming back after remission, about the surgical scars, nausea, and other problems that go with treatments. And they could comfortably discuss their own kinds of cancer and their chances for a future.

Before the first week had passed, Todd wished that the camp were longer than three weeks. He was making friends who would go far away to their own homes when camp was over. Some of them would live to come back another year, but some of them would not. Todd could not forget about his cancer at the camp, but he could really enjoy himself, and that was something he had not done for a very long time. This was especially important to someone who did not know how many more days he had left.

In addition to camps, there are other special programs that bring joy to children who have been cancer patients. For example, there are programs for one-legged skiers, who conquer the slopes with one ski and two poles that have little skis on the ends called outriggers. Groups of these patients, who have lost legs because of bone cancer, participate in an annual trip from the University of Texas M. D. Anderson Hospital in Houston to Winter Park, Colorado, where they take part in a program of skiing, riding down an icy hill on an inner tube, snowmobiling, sleigh rides, and other winter sports. The trip provides patients with an opportunity to prove to themselves that they can overcome obstacles. In trying to master these winter sports, young people build their confidence and conquer their fears. It helps to improve their self-image, an important aspect of rehabilitation.

Wilderness experiences offer new challenges to children who have had cancer. Keith Hopkins, who had a below-the-knee amputation for osteogenic sarcoma, reported that a wilderness program helped him to cope with his cancer better because it helped him to overcome the "why me" part of it and gave him a chance to meet other challenges while facing the biggest challenge of his life.

A number of programs for children with cancer help to grant the wishes of terminally ill children. For example, a ten-year-old boy whose brain cancer was inoperable wanted to visit Disney World, but his parents, who were struggling with large medical bills, could not afford to send him. His dream came true because of volunteers in Rochester's Teddi Project, who staff and fund trips and fulfill other wishes of patients and their families. Begun by the father of Teddi Mervis, who died of a brain tumor, this project is one of a series of programs that reaches out to children with cancer and to their families. Other programs that fulfill wishes of terminally ill children include the Sunshine Foundation in Philadelphia, Pennsylvania, and the Make A Wish Foundation in Phoenix, Arizona.

These are just some of the innovative programs that are helping children with cancer to enjoy their lives in spite of the problems that cancer brings. Although these programs reach only a small percentage of the children whose lives are changed by cancer, they are a big step in the right direction.

9

Looking Toward Tomorrow

Cancer is not a new disease. Doctors have been aware of it for hundreds of years, and the search for clues to its causes has a long history. Perhaps the first awareness of a connection between certain chemicals and cancer in humans came in 1775. In that year, Dr. Percivall Pott of St. Bartholomew's Hospital in London, England, reported on the frequent occurrence of cancer of the skin among boys who were chimney sweeps. Dr. Pott attributed the disease to the contamination of their skin with soot.

About a century after Dr. Pott's observation, an unusually high amount of cancer of the skin was noted among workers in Scottish shale-oil refineries. After that, cancer of the bladder was associated with chemicals used in the dyestuffs industry in Germany. Still later, cancer of the skin was recognized as an occupational disease in the English cotton spinning industry, where workers developed "mule spinner's cancer" believed caused by their association with the mineral oil used for lubrication.

The list of chemicals that might contribute to cancer in humans who are frequently exposed to them has become long and controversial over the years, and additions continue to be made. Questions remain, but some action has been taken to prevent exposure to these possible cancer-causing chemicals, or carcinogens. In 1984, new warnings were approved for cigarette packages in an effort to increase public awareness of the connection between smoking and lung cancer. Continued alarms are being sounded about the presence of potentially dangerous amounts of asbestos in schools and other buildings. But the removal of deadly fibers that flake from ceilings or crumble from insulation and pipes has proceeded at a slow pace. The fact that cancer appears many years after some people begin smoking and that fibers of asbestos lodging in the lungs of children will probably not produce lung cancer or other disease for twenty to thirty years makes accurate research difficult.

The fact that not all smokers and not all children who are exposed to asbestos will develop cancer adds another dimension to the complex problem of cancer research. Why do some children appear to be cancer prone? The problem of why some people seem to be more susceptible to cancer than others intrigues the men and women who search for its causes. The overall incidence of cancer in all societies is estimated to be 25 percent. Why do three out of four people resist cancer?

Although some of the answers to the way cancer develops have been found in the chromosomes of living cells, the genetic material that determines how life develops, there is still much to be learned. Scientists in laboratories throughout the world have been fervently pursuing the link between genes and cancer. Not long ago, several groups of scientists, working independently, discovered the existence of individual genes in the cells of some human cancers that can switch on the cancer process in other normal living cells. The discovery of these genes, called oncogenes or transforming genes, was a great breakthrough in cancer research. They appear to be normal genes that have been harmed during a person's lifetime, although in some cases the genetic error seems to be inherited.

In 1983, scientists of the Leukemia Society of America and Dana-Farber Cancer Institute in Boston found that viral infection like Burkitt's lymphoma causes normal cells to

62

turn into "intermediate" cells that multiply continuously without control. There is always a transforming gene, or genes, in the cell. Acting either independently or together, the genes "turn on" and direct the cells to the final stage of full-blown cancer. Viruses are thought to play a part in only a small percentage of human cancers, however.

Although the presence of genes that have been altered or activated in some way to become cancer genes sets a cell on the road to malignancy, still other factors seem to be involved. The steps that must take place before a cell becomes cancerous may begin when there has been contact with a chemical of the group known as carcinogens. Such a chemical does not cause cancer in its original form, but it undergoes a molecular change in the cell known as activation. This process involves enzymes that cells normally use to convert foreign substances to forms that can be harmlessly excreted. Sometimes, enzymes change the chemical in such a way that it can combine with the genetic material in the cell. People who seem to be cancer prone may have relatively more of the combinations of enzymes that change the carcinogen in such a way that it can enter the cell and bind to the genetic material. When this happens, activation takes place. A step in the sequence that changes a normal cell into a malignancy has thus taken place, but cancer does not necessarily follow.

At this stage, even if activation does take place, the cancer process is usually blocked by repair mechanisms in the cell. But if this mechanism is faulty and the changed gene is not repaired before the cell divides, the offspring of the cell will contain the faulty gene and so will all the cells that are formed when these cells reproduce. Even now, cancer may not follow.

It is quite possible that the faulty gene is one that is inactive. The carcinogen may have bound to any of a cell's 50,000 or so genes, and most of them will not play a part in the cell's turning malignant. In other words, the carcinogen must bind to the right place in order to complete the first step in the development of cancer.

Doctors know that people who have certain rare hereditary diseases are more prone to cancer. For example, in the case of xeroderma pigmentosum, a gene is changed before birth so that the repair mechanism to correct damage from sunlight does not function properly. Victims of this disease have a high degree of skin cancer.

This multistep process may sound complicated enough, but the development of cancer is really far more complex. For example, evidence indicates that more than one altered gene may be needed before malignancy begins. In laboratory mice, at least one gene must be altered, and in many cases more than one is needed to produce cancer. How much chance is there for a cell that already has an altered gene of acquiring another altered gene? Researchers believe that the first set of steps somehow sensitizes the cell to "promoters." Suppose a mouse's skin has been painted with material known to produce cancer in the skin of mice. Usually, no tumor develops, even after a long period of time. In a similar experiment, another mouse's skin is also dosed for a long period of time with certain other chemicals, called promoters. Tumors develop in the treated area. On a third mouse, only promoters are used in the experiment. This mouse does not develop tumors. So it appears that the combination is necessary. Such experiments lead scientists to believe that the appearance of human cancers may involve similar steps.

Since so many complicated processes must occur before a cell becomes malignant, why is cancer so common? The chances that a cell with a damaged gene will become involved in the sequence of events that turn a normal cell into cancer are increased by the fact that the offspring of that cell carry altered genes. The cell with the damaged gene produces many new cells with damaged genes. As their number grows, there is a better chance that one of these cells will be involved in a second set of steps with another carcinogen. Several cycles or repetitions of cycles may have to occur before the right combination of genes exists to produce cells that grow out of control and form a tumor. So it is not surprising to find that some of the children who breathe asbestos in their schools, some of the smokers who inhale, and some of the people exposed to other carcinogens develop cancer only after many years have passed.

Knowledge about how cells become malignant helps researchers develop preventive measures. For example, Harry Gelboin and his colleagues at the National Cancer Institute are working on tests in which a person's enzymes could be profiled. If one could discover which people have an enzyme profile that indicates they are prone to have activation of genes as described above, these people could be encouraged to take special steps to prevent cancer.

Everyone is encouraged to eat foods that may help to block the cancer process and to avoid those foods that appear to promote it. Fiber, fruits, and vegetables in the diet are good; smoked meats, fatty meats, and other fats are bad. Everyone is encouraged to avoid overexposure to sunlight. Warnings about the dangers of smoking and exposure to other toxic chemicals abound.

While scientists continue their all-out assault on cancer, the disease continues to attack people of all ages. At some cancer centers, special emphasis is placed on attacking the kinds of cancer that are more common among young people. The Dana-Farber Cancer Institute, known as the Children's Cancer Research Foundation when it was founded in 1947, was the first organization in the world dedicated exclusively to pediatric cancer research and treatment. Initially supported by the Variety Club of New England and the Boston Braves baseball team, the Institute has grown large and now includes adults, but the public effort popularly known as the Jimmy Fund still makes an important contribution.

At St. Jude's Children's Research Hospital in Memphis, Tennessee, and at laboratories in cancer centers throughout the world, researchers are trying to find new ways to make life longer and better for the many young people who must deal with cancer. Human cancer research is now moving at a faster rate than many experts ever believed possible.

Great volumes of work have been completed in the search for causes and cures of cancer. Attacks have come from many fronts to do battle against the cell lines that are capable of continuous division without relation to bodily needs. Only within recent years have scientists begun to understand the nature of the cancer process at its most fundamental level. As a result, there are outstanding doctors who now hope for the end of cancer within the next fifteen years, rather than the fifty or more that even the most optimistic researchers were once willing to chance as a guess. All researchers are willing to admit that the problem is extremely complex, and sometimes the pieces of the puzzle seem insoluble. But no one knows when a new piece of information will bring new understanding of the switching-on mechanism that now makes the cancer story so bleak for so many. Today, especially in the field of research on cancer as a disease of young people, there is a tremendous sense of hope.

Glossary

acute   occurring over a short period of time, said of a disease that develops quickly.

anemia   a condition in which the blood is deficient in red blood cells, hemoglobin, or total-volume red blood cells. Anemia can be caused by a variety of conditions, such as iron deficiency, infection, and, occasionally leukemia.

antibody   a substance that helps defend the body against infections caused by viruses, bacteria, and other foreign organisms. Antibodies are probably made by lymphocytes.

antigen   a chemical substance that can be recognized by the body as foreign and thus stimulates the body's immune system.

benign tumor   a noncancerous growth, or mass of cells, that does not spread to other parts of the body.

biopsy   the removal and microscopic examination of tissue for purposes of diagnosis.

blast a short name for lymphoblast, an immature white blood cell. Normally, blasts make up less than 5 percent of the cells made by the bone marrow and will grow to form mature white cells. In leukemia, blasts remain immature and accumulate in large numbers in the bone marrow.

bone marrow spongy material that fills the cavities of the bones and is the substance in which many elements of the blood are produced. A doctor may take a small sample from one of the bones in the chest, hip, spine, or leg to determine the condition of the marrow.

cancer a general term that refers to uncontrolled, abnormal growth of cells. The resulting mass is a tumor that can invade and destroy surrounding tissues. In leukemia, the tumor takes on the fluid properties of the blood, the organ it affects.

capillary one of many tiny blood vessels located throughout the body that connect the arteries and the veins. Substances that nourish the cells pass through the capillaries.

carcinogen something that plays a part in causing cancer.

carcinoma cancer of tissues that cover the body (such as the skin or mucous membranes) or tissues that line the internal organs (such as stomach and intestines).

CAT scan computerized axial tomography, a diagnostic X-ray procedure in which a computer is used to generate a three-dimensional image.

CBC complete blood count, a series of tests to examine the makeup of the blood.

cell tiny structure that makes up all the tissues of the body and carries on all the functional activities.

chemotherapy   a form of treatment with drugs that are capable of destroying malignant cells.

chronic   lasting a long time, said of a disease that progresses slowly.

clinical   having to do with the treatment of patients; clinical research is a term applied to information gained from study and treatment of people.

CNS   central nervous system, the brain and spinal cord.

cobalt machine   a machine that administers radiation to tumors.

combination chemotherapy   treatment of an individual cancer patient by the use of two or more anticancer medications.

combination therapy   treatment of an individual cancer patient by the use of two or more methods, such as chemotherapy and surgery.

congenital   any condition existing at birth.

edema   accumulation of fluids within the tissues.

excision   surgical removal of tissue.

finger stick   a procedure in which a small point is opened in the fingertip and a few drops of blood are gathered to do routine blood studies.

gastrointestinal   pertaining to the digestive tract.

glioma   a general term for any of a group of brain or spinal cord cancers.

granulocyte　a certain white blood cell that helps to protect against bacterial infection; granulocytes are also called polys or neutrophils.

hemapheresis　a procedure for donating a portion of the blood, such as white blood cells or platelets, in which the unused portion is returned by transfusion to the donor.

hematocrit　a measure of the total amount of red cells in the blood. The normal hematocrit is 35 percent or more.

hematology　the study of the blood and blood-forming organs.

hematuria　blood in the urine; urine may be pink, red, or brown.

hemoglobin　substance found in red cells that carries oxygen.

hemorrhage　a general term for loss of blood, often profuse, brought about by injury to the blood vessels or by a deficiency of certain necessary blood elements, such as platelets.

Hodgkin's disease　a form of cancer affecting lymphatic and other tissues that play a part in the individual's ability to fight infection.

hormone　a chemical substance that helps regulate the body and is carried by the blood to certain organs from the gland where it is produced.

hyperalimentation see **IVH.**

immune reaction　a reaction of normal tissues to substances recognized as foreign rather than self. The foreign substances can be chemicals, particles, microorganisms, or cells.

immunity   the power that a living organism possesses to resist and overcome infection.

immunotherapy   treatment of a disease by stimulating the body's own defense mechanism against disease.

infection   the invasion and multiplication of disease-producing organisms in the body.

infusion   the continuous slow introduction of a fluid into a vein.

injection   the forcible introduction of liquid into a body part. Injections are IM (intramuscular), into the muscle; IT (intrathecal), into the spinal area; IV (intravenous), into the vein; and SC or sub-q (subcutaneous), just under the skin. Known popularly as a shot.

interferon   a protein normally produced in blood and tissues as a response to viral infection. Interferon manufactured by pharmaceutical firms is used for its antiviral properties and as an anticancer agent in attempts to stop the growth of cancer cells.

irradiate   to treat by exposure to roentgen rays or other radioactive materials.

isotopic scan   a diagnostic procedure for examining the brain, bones, and other organs. A radioactive substance is introduced intravenously, collects in certain organs, and is then studied by special scanners that detect radioactivity.

IVH   intravenous hyperalimentation, total feeding of a patient through the veins, supplying essential nutrients, minerals, and vitamins. It is used in patients who cannot eat for a prolonged period of time.

71

IVP intravenous pyelogram, an X-ray examination of the kidneys that depends on accumulation and visualization in the kidney of a special substance that is injected into a vein.

lesion a change in tissue structure caused by injury or disease. Ulcers, tumors, and abscesses may all be referred to as lesions.

leukemia cancer of the blood forming-tissues (bone marrow, lymph nodes, spleen) characterized by overproduction of white cells. **Lymphocytic leukemia** is cancer in the lymph cells of the bone marrow. **Nonlymphocytic leukemia,** or **myelogenous leukemia,** is cancer of the nonlymphocytic white cells of the bone marrow.

leukocyte white blood cell.

lumbar puncture spinal tap, a routine technique for removing a small amount of the fluid that bathes the brain and spinal cord. In patients suffering from leukemia, this fluid is tested for the possible presence of blast cells as well as other elements.

lymph a nearly colorless fluid that bathes body cells and moves through the lymphatic vessels of the body.

lymphangiography an X-ray procedure using a radiopaque dye to examine the lymph system.

lymph node bean-shaped structure found scattered along vessels of the lymphatic system. Lymph nodes act as filters, collecting bacteria or cancer cells that may travel through the lymphatic system. In leukemia, they enlarge when filled with lymphoblasts.

lymphocyte white blood cell responsible for the production of antibodies and for the direct destruction of invading organisms or cancer cells.

lymphoma   malignant growths of lymph nodes. Burkitt's lymphoma is a cancer of the lymph nodes often found in the abdomen and occasionally in the jaw.

malignant tumor   a tumor made of cancer cells.

marrow transplant   a procedure in which the patient's bone marrow is replaced, usually with healthy bone marrow from a compatible relative. When the patient is given back his or her own treated bone marrow, the procedure is referred to as autologous.

melanoma   a pigmented form of cancer of the skin. The tumor may vary in color from nearly black to almost white.

metastasis   the spread of cancer from its original site.

monocyte   one type of white blood cell that destroys invading bacteria.

neoplasm   a new growth of different or abnormal tissue; tumor.

neuroblastoma   cancer of a part of the nervous system other than the brain or spinal cord.

neutrophil   a type of white blood cell that plays a major role in the body's defense against bacteria, viruses, and fungi.

nodule   a small mass of tissue or tumor.

noninvasive   not involving cutting or puncturing the skin or inserting or injecting anything into the patient; said of diagnostic procedures.

nuclear medicine the field of medicine dealing with the administration of radioactive materials for the diagnosis of disease and the treatment of certain cancers.

oncogene a gene associated with cancer.

oncologist a physician or scientist specializing in the study of cancer.

oncology study of the physical, chemical, and biological properties and features of cancer.

osteosarcoma cancer of the cells in the bone.

pathology the branch of medicine involved in making diagnoses from the examination of tissues.

plasma the liquid portion of the blood in which the cells and elements are suspended. It contains proteins and minerals necessary for normal body functioning.

platelet one of the main components of the blood, which forms clots that seal injured areas and prevent hemorrhage.

prognosis an estimate of the outcome of a disease, a prediction.

prosthesis an artificial structure designed to replace a missing body part.

protocol the plan of treatment for a specific case.

rad the unit of measurement of a radiation dose.

radiation therapy a treatment based on the capacity of X-rays to destroy malignant cells.

74

red blood cell   a cell that contains hemoglobin and carries oxygen to the tissues.

regression   reduction or disappearance of cancerous tissue, usually as a result of therapy.

relapse   return of a disease after its initial improvement.

remission   complete or partial disappearance of the signs and symptoms of a disease, the period during which a disease is under control. Partial remission in leukemia refers to a condition in which most leukemia cells have been destroyed but some blasts are still present in the bone marrow or blood. Complete remission is the disappearance of all detectable blasts.

retinoblastoma   cancer of the retina of the eye.

rhabdomyosarcoma   cancer in the muscle cells.

sarcoma   a cancer of connective tissue, bone cartilage, fat, muscle, nerve sheath, blood vessels, or lymphoid system.

scan   picture of an organ or part of the body such as the liver, brain, or specific bones, obtained by using X-rays or radioactivity.

spinal tap   see **lumbar puncture.**

staging   test done in an attempt to define the extent of cancer.

subcutaneous   beneath the skin.

symptom   feeling of illness experienced by an individual that indicates disease or infection.

syndrome a set of symptoms that commonly occur together.

therapeutic pertaining to treatment.

therapy treatment of a disease. With cancer patients, **induction therapy** is an initial treatment designed to obtain remission; **maintenance therapy** is the treatment used to kill any remaining cancer cells and avoid a relapse after the cancer has been successfully reduced to an undetectable level; **supportive therapy** is any care not directly concerned with treating the disease itself, such as nutrition supplements and blood transfusions.

tissue a collection of cells that are similar in structure and function.

tomography a technique of diagnosis that uses X-ray photographs in which the shadows of structures before and behind the section being studied do not show.

toxicity a word used to describe undesirable side effects caused by a drug.

transducer a small hand-held instrument used to locate tumors by sound waves.

tumor any abnormal growth in a localized area.

vein a vessel carrying blood from the tissues that is relatively lacking in oxygen.

Wilms' tumor a form of cancer of the kidney.

X-rays high-energy radiation used in high doses to treat cancer or in low doses to diagnose disease.

Suggested Reading

Middle Grades

Bach, Alice. *Waiting for Johnny Miracle*. Harper & Row, 1980.

Baker, Lynn S. *You and Leukemia: A Day at a Time*, rev. ed. W. B. Saunders Co., 1978.

Bernstein, Joanne, and Stephen V. Gullo. *Loss and How to Cope with It*. Seabury Press. 1977.

Fox, Ray Errol. *Angelo Ambrosia*. Alfred A. Knopf, 1979.

Greenberg, Jan. *No Dragons to Slay*. Farrar, Straus, 1983.

Gunther, John. *Death Be Not Proud*. Harper & Row, 1971.

Hyde, Margaret O., and Lawrence E. Hyde. *Cloning and the New Genetics*. Enslow Publishers, 1984.

Ipswitch, Elaine. *Scott Was Here*. Delacorte Press, 1979.

Jampolsky, Gerald G., and Pat Taylor, eds. *There Is a Rainbow Behind Every Dark Cloud*. Center for Attitudinal Healing, 1978.

—— and Gloria Murray, eds. *Another Look at the Rainbow: Straight from the Siblings*. Center for Attitudinal Healing, 1982.

Lancaster, Matthew. *Hang Toughf*. Hang Toughf, 1983.

High School

Alsop, Stewart. *Stay of Execution*. J. B. Lippincott Co., 1973.

Lund, Doris. *Eric*. J. B. Lippincott Co., 1974.

Further Information

National Organizations

The following groups offer educational materials (usually free) and, in some cases, limited financial assistance and support services. You may call or write for further information.

THE AMERICAN CANCER SOCIETY
National Headquarters
777 Third Avenue
New York, NY 10017
Ask for a list of local divisions.
212-371-2900

THE CANDLELIGHTERS CHILDHOOD CANCER
   FOUNDATION
Suite 1011
2025 Eye Street, NW
Washington, DC 20006
202-659-5136
Write for free copy of the Youth Newsletter.

LEUKEMIA SOCIETY OF AMERICA
National Headquarters
800 Second Avenue
New York, NY 10017
212-573-8484
Or contact the local chapter listed in your telephone directory.

CANADIAN CANCER SOCIETY
Société Canadienne du Cancer
Suite 1001
130 Bloor Street West
Toronto, Ontario M5S 2V7
Or contact your Provincial chapter.

Comprehensive Cancer Centers

The following institutions are recognized by the National Cancer Institute and have met rigorous criteria imposed by the National Cancer Advisory Board.

ALABAMA

University of Alabama in
  Birmingham
Comprehensive Cancer Center
Lurleen Wallace Tumor
  Institute
1824 6th Avenue South
Birmingham, AL 35294
(205) 934-5077

CALIFORNIA

University of Southern California
Comprehensive Cancer
  Center
1441 Eastlake Avenue
Los Angeles, CA 90033-0804
(213) 224-6416

UCLA-Jonsson Comprehensive Cancer Center
Louis Factor Health Sciences
  Bldg.
10833 LeConte Avenue
Los Angeles, CA 90024
(213) 825-5268

CONNECTICUT

Yale Comprehensive Cancer
  Center
Yale University School of
  Medicine
333 Cedar Street
New Haven, CT 06510
(203) 785-4095

Georgetown University/
Howard University
Comprehensive Cancer Center

Vincent T. Lombardi Cancer
  Research Center
Georgetown University
  Medical Center
3800 Reservoir Road, N.W.
Washington, DC 20007
(202) 625-7721

Howard University Cancer
  Research Center
College of Medicine
Department of Oncology
2041 Georgia Avenue, N.W.
Washington, DC 20060
(202) 636-7697

FLORIDA

Comprehensive Cancer Center
  for the State of Florida
University of Miami School of
  Medicine
1475 N.W. 12th Avenue
Miami, FL 33101
(305) 545-7707

ILLINOIS

Illinois Cancer Council
36 South Wabash Avenue,
Suite 700
Chicago, IL 60603
(312) 346-9813

Northwestern University
  Cancer Center
303 East Chicago Avenue
Chicago, IL 60611
(312) 266-5250

University of Chicago Cancer
  Research Center
950 East 59th Street
Chicago, IL 60637
(312) 962-6180

University of Illinois
  Department of Surgery,
  Division of Surgical
Oncology
840 South Wood Street
Chicago, IL 60612
(312) 996-6666

Rush Cancer Center
Suite 820
1725 West Harrison Street
Chicago, IL 60612
(312) 942-6028

MARYLAND

Johns Hopkins Oncology
  Center
600 North Wolfe Street
Baltimore, MD 21205
(301) 955-8822

MASSACHUSETTS

Dana-Farber Cancer Institute
44 Binney Street
Boston, MA 02115
(617) 732-3555

MICHIGAN

Michigan Cancer Foundation
Meyer L. Prentis Cancer
  Center
110 East Warren Avenue
Detroit, MI 48201
(313) 833-0710

81

MINNESOTA

Mayo Clinic
200 First Street, S.W.
Rochester, MN 55905
(507) 284-8964

NEW YORK

Columbia University Cancer
  Research Center
701 West 168th Street,
  Rm. 1208
New York, NY 10032
(212) 694-3647

Memorial Sloan-Kettering
  Cancer Center
1275 York Avenue
New York, NY 10021
(212) 794-6561

Roswell Park Memorial
  Institute
666 Elm Street
Buffalo, NY 14263
(716) 845-5770

NORTH CAROLINA

Duke Comprehensive Cancer
  Center
P.O. Box 3814
Duke University Medical
  Center
Durham, NC 27710
(919) 684-2282

OHIO

Ohio State University Comprehensive Cancer Center
Suite 302
410 West 12th Avenue
Columbus, OH 43210
(614) 422-5022

PENNSYLVANIA

Fox Chase/University of
  Pennsylvania Cancer Center

The Fox Chase Cancer Center
7701 Burholme Avenue
Philadelphia, PA 19111
(215) 728-2781

University of Pennsylvania
  Cancer Center
3400 Spruce Street
7th Floor, Silverstein Pavilion
Philadelphia, PA 19104
(215) 662-3910

TEXAS

The University of Texas
  System Cancer Center
M.D. Anderson Hospital and
  Tumor Institute
6723 Bertner Avenue
Houston, TX 77030
(713) 792-6000

WASHINGTON

Fred Hutchinson Cancer
  Research Center
1124 Columbia Street
Seattle, WA 98104
(206) 292-2930 or 292-7545

WISCONSIN

Wisconsin Clinical Cancer
  Center
University of Wisconsin
Department of Human
  Oncology
600 Highland Avenue
Madison, WI 53792
(608) 263-8610

Other Resources

Contact the Office of Cancer Communications, National Cancer Institute, Building 31, Room 4B39, Bethesda, MD 20205 for free or inexpensive publications about cancer and young people. Four useful booklet titles are:

Diet and Nutrition:
A Resource for Parents of Children with Cancer

Chemotherapy and You:
A Guide to Self-Help During Treatment

Help Yourself:
Tips for Teenagers with Cancer

Young People with Cancer

Telephone Information Service

The Cancer Information Service provides answers to questions without charge. By dialing the proper number, you will be automatically connected to the service for your area. The Cancer Information Service is administered by the National Cancer Institute, and most of its offices are associated with Comprehensive Cancer Centers.

Cancer Information Service offices do not diagnose cancer or recommend treatment for individual cases. They do provide support, understanding, and rapid access to the latest information on cancer and on local resources.

Dial 1-800-4-CANCER except as follows:

Alaska: 1-800-638-6070

Washington, D.C., and suburbs in Maryland and Virginia: 636-5700

Oahu: 524-1234 (neighboring islands call collect)

New York City: 794-7982

Spanish-speaking staff members are available to callers in the following areas, daytime hours only: California (area codes 213, 714, 619, and 805), Florida, Georgia, Illinois, northern New Jersey, New York City, and Texas.

Camps for Children with Cancer and Their Siblings

ARIZONA

Camp Sunrise
Division Director of Medical
  Affairs
ACS Arizona Division
P.O. Box 33187
Phoenix, AZ 85067

One-week medically staffed program for children 7–15 funded by American Cancer Society; transportation provided.

CALIFORNIA

Camp Ronald McDonald for
  Good Times
c/o Pepper Abrams
201 North Carmelina Avenue
Los Angeles, CA 90040

Two six-day sessions for children 8 up and young adults now or previously treated for cancer; medically staffed.

Camp Okizu
c/o Coral Cotten, Director of
  Camping
Alameda-Contra Costa Council
  of Camp Fire
1201 East 14th Street
Oakland, CA 94606

One-week oncology camp for children with life-threatening illnesses; oral medications given.

Camp Reach for the Sky
c/o Ann Buckley
ACS California Division
2251 San Diego Avenue, Suite
  B 150
San Diego, CA 92110

Five-day overnight camp.

Camp Sunburst
c/o Geri Brooks, Executive
  Camp Director
  Columbia Pacific University
    Foundation
150 Shoreline
Mill Valley, CA 94941

Two-week summer residential program for chronically ill children 6–16.

COLORADO

Sky High Hope Camp
c/o Nancy King, RN,
  Camp Director
2430 East Arkansas Avenue
Denver, CO 80210

One-week camp for children 8–17 who have or have had leukemia or cancer.

CONNECTICUT

Camp Rising Sun
(Hemlocks Outdoor Education
  Center)
c/o Carolyn Butler
6 Glen Hill Lane
Wilton, CT 06897

Overnight program for children 6–18; physician and nurse available.

or c/o Richard Smith, MSW,
ACSW
Yale New Haven Hospital
20 York Street
New Haven, CT 06504

or c/o Jane Bemis
ACS Connecticut Division
P.O. Box 410
Wallingford, CT 06492

FLORIDA

R.O.C.K. Camp (Lake Wales Camp)
c/o Beverly Deason
ACS Florida Division
1001 South MacDill Avenue
Tampa, FL 33709

Two-week overnight camp for children 7–17.

GEORGIA

Camp Sunshine
c/o CURE
P.O. Box 1321
Lawrenceville, GA 30246

One-week medically staffed camp for Georgia children and adolescents who have had leukemia or other forms of cancer.

IDAHO

Camp Betchacan
c/o Pam Smith
ACS Idaho Division
P.O. Box 5386
Boise, ID 83705

Medically staffed camp for children with cancer and siblings.

ILLINOIS

One Step at a Time Camp
c/o Children's Oncology
   Services of Illinois
120 South Lasalle Street
Chicago, IL 60603

Two one-week sessions for children with cancer from Illinois and Wisconsin.

The Dream Factory Camp
c/o Arthur A. H. Nehring,
   Director
R.R. 2, Box 277
Pinckneyville, IL 62274

One-week overnight camp.

Summer Sunrise
c/o Deb Wetherbee
Maine Niles Association of
   Special Recreation
7640 Main Street
Niles, IL 60648

Day camp at Parkview School for children with cancer and siblings 4–10; oncology nurse on duty.

87

TLC (Together Through Love
and Caring) Camp
c/o Nancy Kohl
Lombard Junior Women's Club
Lombard, IL 60148

One-week day camp for children 5–12 with cancer or leukemia. Staffed by oncology
nurses.

INDIANA

The Little Red Door
Marion County Cancer Society
United Cancer Council
1803 North Meridian Street
Indianapolis, IN 46202

One-week summer camp for
cancer patients 8–18.

IOWA

Camp Amanda
c/o JoAnn Zimmerman
Catholic Council for Social
Concern
700 3rd Street
Des Moines, IA 50309

Weekend program for chil-
dren who have lost family
member to cancer, other diseases, or accidents.

KANSAS

Camp Hope
c/o Norma Meddendorf, MSW
ACS Kansas Division
3003 Van Buren
Topeka, KS 66611

One-week free camp for 50
children; medically staffed.

KENTUCKY

Indian Summer Camp
c/o Darlo Tanner
469 Longbranch Road
Union, KY 41091

One-week summer program
for children 7–17 with leukemia and other cancer; medical
personnel available for chemotherapy, blood counts, and
emergencies.

MICHIGAN

Special Days Summer Camp
c/o Steve Farris
1340 Wines Drive
Ann Arbor, MI 48103

One-week summer camp for
children 8–18 with cancer;
winter weekend camp is also
held.

MINNESOTA

Camp Courage
c/o Sandy Miller
3801 Yates North
Crystal, MN 55422

Six-day session for pediatric oncology patients 7–13.

MISSOURI

Kiwanis Camp Wyman
Contact local Kiwanis Club
  or hospital for information.

Eleven-day summer program for children with cancer; financial assistance available.

NEW JERSEY

Camp Happy Times
c/o Sy Frankel, Valerie Fund
40 Somerset Street
Plainfield, NJ 07060

One-week medically staffed camp for children from New York and New Jersey treatment centers.

Happiness Is Camping
c/o Murray Struver, Gramercy
  Boy's Club
2169 Grand Concourse
Bronx, NY 10453

One-week session for children with cancer,, including leukemia; medical staff for chemotherapy and blood counts.

NEW MEXICO

c/o World College
Las Vegas, NM 87701

NEW YORK

BEST (Brothers and Sisters
  Together)
c/o Polly Schwensen
University of Rochester Medical
  Center
P.O. Box 650
Rochester, NY 14642

Weekend program for siblings 7–17 of children with cancer.

Camp Good Days and Special
  Times
c/o Gary Mervis, Director
P.O. Box 245
Pittsfield, NY 14534

For children with cancer whose illness is either in remission or under control with oral chemotherapy.

Happiness Is Camping
See NEW JERSEY

Camp Open Arms
c/o United Cancer Council
1441 East Avenue
Rochester, NY 14610

Two-week day camp for children with cancer and blood diseases and their siblings or friends.

NORTH CAROLINA

Camp Rainbow
c/o Brenda Martin, MSW
East Carolina School of
    Medicine
Greenville, NC 27834

One-week medically staffed camp free to eastern North Carolina pediatric cancer patients 5–18.

OHIO

Children's Hospital Hematology
    Camp
c/o Jim Miser, M.D.
Children's Hospital
700 Children's Drive
Columbus, OH 43205

One weekend program.

Camp Friendship—Camp Kern
c/o Powell R. Zeit, M.D.,
    Director
ACS Ohio Division
1375 Euclid Avenue
Cleveland, OH 44115

One-week camp.

Indian Summer Camp
See KENTUCKY

OKLAHOMA

Fun in the Sun & Fun in the
    Fall
c/o Marianne B. Jost, POSW
Oklahoma Children's Memorial
    Hospital
940 NE 13th Street
Oklahoma City, OK 73104

No-charge Friday–Sunday program limited to children in therapy; medically staffed.

Camp Waluhili
c/o Peggy Jacks, Camp Director
Camp Fire, Inc.
5305 East 41st Street
Tulsa, OK 74135

Special one-week oncology session for children 7 and older; medically staffed.

PENNSYLVANIA

Camp Can-Do
c/o Kathy Nelson, RN
Children's Hospital of
  Pittsburgh
125 DeSoto Street
Pittsburgh, PA 15213

For children 8–14 who have been treated or who are currently being treated for cancer; medically staffed.

Camp Dost
c/o Paul Kettlewell, M.D.
Geisinger Medical Center
Danville, PA 17822

One-week summer program for cancer patients 8–18; medically staffed.

SOUTH CAROLINA

Camp Kemo
c/o Frances Friedman, Director
Richland Memorial Hospital
3301 Harden Street
Columbia, SC 29203

One-week overnight camp.

Camp Happy Days
c/o Debby Stephenson
7821 Dorchester Road
Charleston, SC 29418

TENNESSEE

Camp Eagle's Nest
c/o East Tennessee Children's
  Hospital
Knoxville, TN 37901

For children 6–18 from the East Tennessee Children's Hospital Oncology/Hematology Clinic; co-sponsored by Xerox.

Camp Remission   One-week overnight camp.
c/o Leila Rust, Director of
  Service
ACS Tennessee Division
713 Melpark Drive
Nashville, TN 37204

TEXAS

Candelighters Camp   Medically staffed camp for
  Courageous   children with cancer 7–18.
P.O. Box 31146   Some financial aid available.
El Paso, TX 79931

Camp Esperanza   Free one-week program for
c/o Sally Francis   children 6–16 who have or
Children's Medical Center   have had cancer; medically
1935 Amelia   staffed.
Dallas, TX 75235

Camp Periwinkle   Free one-week medically
c/o Judly Packler or Elsie   staffed camp for children 6–16
  McDermott   currently being treated at
Research Hematology   Texas Children's Hospital;
Texas Children's Hospital   transportation provided.
Houston, TX 77030

Camp Sanguinity
c/o Ellen North, Camp Director
Cook Children's Hospital
1212 West Lancaster Avenue
Fort Worth, TX 76102

Camp Star Trails
c/o Jan Johnson
M. D. Anderson Hospital and
  Tumor Institute
6723 Bertner
Houston, TX 77030

Camp Discovery
ACS Texas Division
Professional Pediatric
  Committee
8214 Wurzbach Road
San Antonio, TX 78229

UTAH

Camp Kostopulos
c/o Miles Shepherd
  or Ellen Eckels
ACS Utah Division
610 East South Temple
Salt Lake City, UT 84102

Medically staffed camp for children with cancer and their siblings.

VIRGINIA

Camp Fantastic
c/o Tom Baker, Special Love
P.O. Box 3243
Winchester, VA 22601

One-week overnight camp for children with cancer 8–16, counselor training program for those over 16; staffed by NCI medical personnel.

Camp Holiday Trails
P.O. Box 5806
Charlottesville, VA 22903

Therapeutic camping experience for children with special health needs.

WASHINGTON

Camp Bet'U Can
ACS Washington Division
P.O. Box 1362
Richland, WA 99352

Medically staffed camp sponsored by the American Cancer Society.

CANADA

Camp Magic Moments
c/o Judy Steen
McDonald's Restaurants of
  Canada
20 Eglinton Avenue West
Toronto, Ontario, Canada
  M4R 2E6

Index